PRIMER OF TOWING

Old steam tug towing barkentine across the bar.

Primer of Towing

George H. Reid

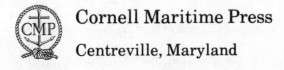

Cornell Maritime Press

Centreville, Maryland

Library of Congress Cataloging in Publication Data

Reid, George H   1924—

   Primer of towing.
   Includes Index.
   1. Tugboats.   2. Towing.   3. Towboats.   I. Title.
VM464.R44   623.88′2′32   75-38648
ISBN 0-87033-212-0

Manufactured in the United States of America

First edition, 1975; third printing, 1984

Contents

Page

Preface vii

1. An Introduction to Towing 1

2. The Tug 6

3. The Barge 11

4. Gear and Rigging for Coastwise and Ocean Towing 16

5. Ship Work 30

6. Barge Handling 41

7. Making and Breaking Tow 48

8. The Multiple Tow 53

9. Inland and River Towing 59

10. The Tug at Sea 65

11. Salvage and Rescue 71

12. Anchor Work 79

13. Handling the Big, Big Barge 82

14. Tips on Towing 87

Index 93

To Evelin

Preface

A distinguished author and educator once pointed out that "one only has to go to the library to become the second-best authority on any given subject." His observation was, perhaps, made facetiously, but served to emphasize the fact that there is a wealth of information available on almost anything of interest.

Unfortunately, in spite of the considerable amount of written material devoted to seamanship and its kindred arts, its application to towing operations has been largely overlooked, and those of us who chose to sail on tugboats were obliged to acquire our skills through "experience."

"Experience" is essential, and there are no short cuts to genuine competence, but "word of mouth" and "trial and error" are tedious ways of learning, and for those of us working in the towing industry there has never been an alternative.

I can recall many occasions in the past when I wished that I had access to someone else's experience in order to solve a particular problem. I hope the following chapters in this volume may be a source of information for others who find themselves in similar straits.

As indicated by the title, this book is a "primer." The individual must still develop his proficiency by engaging in the various activities required in this field of marine endeavour.

I must acknowledge my debt to my mentors in the past who gave me sound counsel. I also appreciate the shared experiences and advice I have received from other seafarers with whom I've had contact through the years.

But my decision to write something on the subject of towing stemmed mostly from the experience I gained teaching newcomers the "tricks of the trade." This association, in most instances, proved mutually illuminating for it was through them that I learned what beginners needed to know, and therein lies the purpose of this book—to provide a basic knowledge of towing.

GEORGE H. REID

Chapter 1

An Introduction to Towing

The purpose here is to provide some insight into the mechanics of towing. While my efforts are directed principally toward the seaman or ship's officer who might have some professional interest in the subject, it is also hoped that the pleasure boatman, or landsman with inquiring mind, might find this information to be of interest.

The field of towing and tugboat operations is extensive and practices vary greatly in different parts of the country. In spite of this, the basics are much the same wherever one goes, and I hope to provide sufficient information to enable those aspiring to this line of work to enter it with a sound knowledge of the fundamentals.

The genealogy of present-day towing dates back to 1802 when a small steam tug, the *Charlotte Dundas*, was constructed. It was built with the hope that it would prove more efficient than the horses then in use for towing barges in the Forth and Clyde Canal. On its trial run the small vessel successfully towed two barges at a speed of about three knots. However, it was feared that the wash from the paddle wheel would damage the banks of the canal with the result that the vessel was laid up and allowed to rot. The ice had been broken, however, and by the middle of the 1830's steam tugs were becoming common in ports of more industrialized European countries. A painting by J.M.W. Turner entitled "The Fighting Temeraire" shows a famous "old ship of the line" of Admiral Nelson's day on her way to the ship breakers in tow of a side-wheel steam tug. Aside from the dated appearance of the vessels, it is a commonplace scene likely to be encountered on any waterway today. The painting was executed in 1838.

By the 1850's the steam tug was encountered in major ports throughout the world. The acceptance of the steam tug had a profound effect upon the entire maritime industry. It not only spurred trade and transport on inland waters, but encouraged the shipwrights and shipping companies to explore the potential of sail to the extent they did. Prior to the advent of the steam tug, the size of ocean sailing vessels was restricted by practical considerations. They could only be shifted about in confined waters by warping or by the use of pulling boats. The great ships and barques that plied the trade routes of the world from the middle 19th Century through the early 20th Century would have fared badly in these circumstances, and many ports of the world would have been off limits to them without assistance from tugs.

1

During this epoch it became customary for tugs to stand offshore at busy ports in hopes of giving a tow to an arriving windjammer. This was a tough and competitive business, and the fee for towing was based largely on what the traffic would bear.

It is worth noting that the steam engine, which had been such a positive factor in the development of sail, would ultimately be the cause of its decline. But steam, too, has gone the way of sail—at least on tugs. The new compact diesel has replaced steam as a source of power. Now the steam tug seems to have joined the clipper ship, fondly remembered but seen only as a relic of times past.

A tug is a floating power plant. It needs only to be big enough to provide an adequate base for her machinery and strong enough to withstand the rigors of her trade. A tug's crew is small and requires little space. An oceangoing tug of 100' or so in length and 1800 h.p. would normally have a crew of about eight men. Therefore, a tug's size is, to a large extent, indicated by considerations of fuel capacity and seaworthiness. Long-haul tugs are of generous proportions for these reasons. Under the U.S. flag, extremely large tugs are uncommon as they become subject to the same manning and licensing requirements of a much larger vessel and are, therefore, uneconomical to operate. Most tugs under the U.S. flag are usually less than 200 gross tons, and few over 300 gross tons are encountered.

While the majority of tugs are originally built for towing, it is not unusual to see vessels successfully employed in this operation which were originally constructed for some other type of service. Among the converts one could list former minesweepers, tuna clippers, shrimpers, Coast Guard cutters and buoy tenders. Even some small freighters have wound up in the towing business. While it must be admitted that they seldom prove as efficient and able as a vessel built specifically for towing, they do serve their purpose.

Prime towing requirements are pulling power and good maneuverability, and a vessel possessing these characteristics can sometimes do quite well even though towing may not have been considered in the original plans.

Towing has kept apace of advances taking place in other areas of the Merchant Marine, but in spite of this it is apparent that the full potential has not been reached. Tugs everywhere are engaging in more diverse activities and towing companies are looking beyond the limitations of their present equipment. Transoceanic voyages are commonplace nowadays; dredges, drill rigs, floating dry docks, and ships to be scrapped are just a few of the many varied pieces of equipment that reach their destination at the end of some tug's tow hawser.

Large or unwieldy objects may be shipped more conveniently and cheaply by tug and barge than by steamer. In some cases a barge designed to carry a cargo not compatible with other cargoes may lay up, but the tug is free to seek other employment to relieve the cost of the operation.

The evolutionary process that has enhanced a present-day tug's capabilities has been stimulated by needs of new industries as well as the conventional freighter's present inability to compete for low freight cargoes over short routes. It would be tedious to attempt to list all of these developments of recent years but some should be mentioned as they are too important to ignore.

1. *Propulsion.* The principal factor is the availability of light and powerful diesel engines which have almost completely replaced steam due to the former's more favorable weight to horsepower ratio and the increased range capability for a given fuel capacity.

2. *Power Transmission.* Most tugs being built today are equipped with some type of clutch and many have wheelhouse controls. This does away with the main objection to diesel power: the occasional failure to start when going from ahead to astern or vice versa with the direct reversing type engine. The amount of maneuvering was often restricted due to a lack of volume in their air tanks as well.

3. *Towing Gear.* The development of new synthetic fiber hawsers has certainly been a major boon for the towing industry. Nylon has proved to be about the best hawser material one could hope for—used by itself or in conjunction with a tow cable. It is roughly three times as strong as manila of the same diameter, tremendously elastic, resistant to wear, and does not rot or mildew. Other synthetics are better for working lines, handling barges alongside and for harbor services; nylon is too elastic for these purposes. The new high-tensile steel cables for towing are worth mentioning, for without towing gear of sufficient strength, the new high-horsepower diesel engines would be useless.

4. *Propeller and Rudder Design.* The refinements in propeller design, the development of practical and reliable controllable pitch propellers, as well as the development of the Kort nozzle and flanking rudders are of major importance in utilizing the power of today's modern engines. Although propeller design has kept apace with the advancements of the industry, the controllable pitch wheel is probably the most effective in converting engine torque into thrust as its pitch can be adjusted for various load conditions, just as one would shift gears on a car. This works out well for long tows but is somewhat unhandy in situations requiring a lot of rapid maneuvering. The Kort nozzle has won general acceptance on large inland pusher tugs on western rivers, usually with flanking rudders used in conjunction with it, to aid maneuverability. The Kort nozzle is an airfoil shaped sleeve fitted around the propeller. The word "nozzle" adequately describes its effect. This is reliably reported to increase the propeller thrust about 40 percent. It is

less commonly used on offshore tugs, and is then frequently used as a pivoting unit, i.e., as a Kort nozzle and rudder combined.

If the many 10- to 20,000-ton barges now in service (together with the 3000 and 5000 h.p. tugs necessary to tow them) are any indication, it would seem towing has at last become a full-fledged member of the United States Merchant fleet rather than a mere auxiliary.

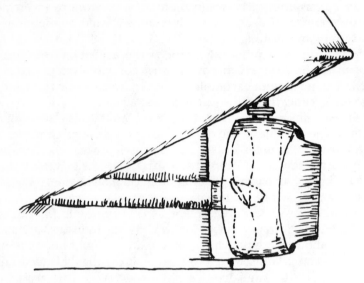

Kort nozzle rudder on tug.

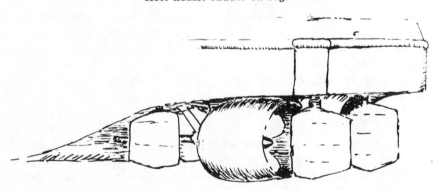

Kort nozzles on river towboat with flanking rudders.

With exceptions towing tends to fall into one of three main categories: harbor work, inland and river, ocean and coastwise. Some tugs may be employed in all three types of work, while others will be used exclusively in one phase or another. Consequently, personnel employed may be familiar with only one type of operation. Should the vessel's employment change, the crew will make out better than the completely uninitiated but not as well as those with a broader background. In most situations the tug captains and mates will be highly skilled at handling their tugs and tows.

My intent is not to embark on a course in shiphandling, but it should be pointed out that in no other work (except piloting) is this skill so essential. While this skill may be acquired by practically anyone, some will learn more rapidly than others. Small-boat experience is probably the best way to gain a knowledge of the fundamentals. The average ship's officer on freighters is usually not too well prepared in this respect since, unless he has been sailing as master, he will have had little opportunity to do any maneuvering.

I feel that shiphandling is more readily learned than taught and though many books treat the subject exhaustively and well, only actual practice in handling a vessel will develop the necessary proficiency. Companies operating tugs are well aware of this and usually are prepared to invest sufficient time in a promising prospect to allow him to acquire the necessary experience. A background as a seaman is the best recommendation, as seamanship is basic even though the application is different.

Chapter 2

The Tug

Tugs vary in size and shape, often being pram- or scow-shaped for inland service, and ranging in horsepower from about 200 h.p. to 7—8000 h.p.

Some shipyards construct stock sizes ranging from a minimum of about 40' to 95' or more. These will have varying power options to suit the potential purchaser.

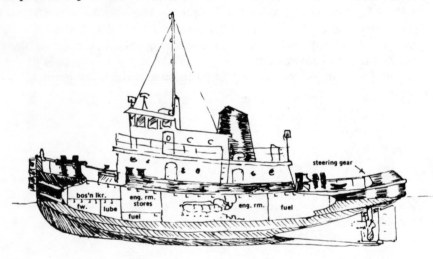

Typical general purpose tug for limited ocean, coastwise and general harbor service.

Smaller tugs are often built with a specific purpose in mind—some for dredge tenders, others for handling small barges, and as general auxiliary vessels. The present trend for larger tugs is to build versatile vessels physically able to go to sea, with enough fuel capacity to make lengthy voyages. Original construction costs are higher in all-purpose boats, but the variety of work they can engage in justifies this.

The modern tug, either single- or twin-screw, is generally more full-bodied than older boats, with a beam length ratio of about 3.5:1. Twin-screw tugs are becoming more common due to their excellent maneuverability and the backup in case one engine fails.

A tug's hull is usually overbuilt by conventional standards. Towing is really the "contact sport" of the maritime industry, and the additional

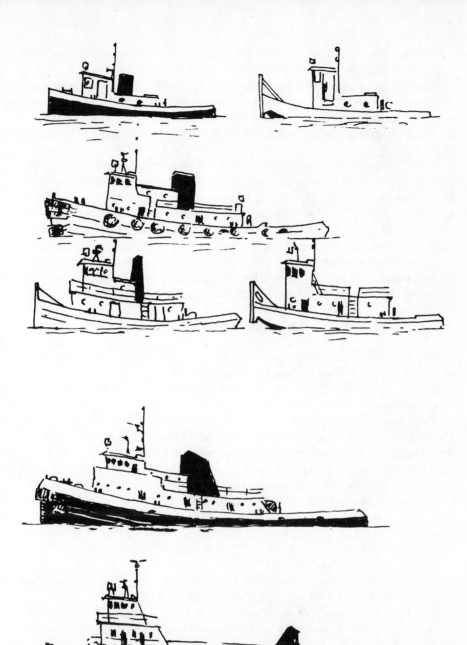

Examples of tugs and towboats encountered on major waterways.

"beef" in the hull helps them withstand the frequent heavy contacts common in this type of work.

Tugs doing much ship work should have fairly narrow wheelhouses and masts that can be lowered easily in order to work alongside vessels with considerable flare without being damaged. Despite this, the flare is so great in many cases that a certain amount of damage to the tug is inevitable.

A tug's bulwarks are normally tumbled home and there will usually be split-pipe rubrails running fore and aft on the freeboard to stiffen and protect the hull. There will be heavy bitts forward, tow bitts aft, and quarter bitts located fore and aft on either side. The bitts must be large enough to properly belay the large-size working lines required on tugs, and must be well secured to the deck to insure that they bear up under the heavy strains placed on them. The towing bitts are customarily built well forward of the rudders so that the tug can pivot.

As noted elsewhere, vessels originally designed for another type of work may occasionally be seen engaged in towing, and most of them will have had their bitts beefed up and their hull strengthened in critical areas.

Fair size tugs generally have an after control station to enable the skipper to keep a close eye on the hawser while heaving in or putting up a towline on a ship. There should be a searchlight aft as well, and a line to the whistle is also a help.

Tugs have little reserve buoyance in comparison to cargo vessels. Most have relatively limited freeboard and below-deck areas may consist largely of fuel and water tanks, and machinery spaces. The main flotation source on a tug may well be the engine room. For this reason a tug can be quite vulnerable if holed in this area.

In many cases the generators, panel boards and pumps are located so low that they will be knocked out of action before the water has risen much above the engine-room floor plate. If this situation exists, an auxiliary pump complete with foot valve strainer, hoses, etc., should be kept on board as a safety measure. The pump should be driven by its own engine, preferably diesel. Gas will suffice if the proper precautions are taken with regard to stowing it and its spare fuel.

The income of the towing business is a derivative of the horsepower developed by the main engine. More often than not, revenue earned is directly related to this, and it is common to charter out a tug based either on its horsepower or its Bollard pull. Bollard pull is simply a way of stating the amount of force a tug can exert on a static pull. Ordinarily a tug is expected to exert approximately one ton of Bollard pull for each 100 horsepower that the main engine develops. Tugs with a favorable bottom configuration will develop much more thrust as will tugs equipped with a Kort nozzle.

While a tug's horsepower is a fair criterion of its capability, it is worth noting that a small tug with big horsepower may outpull a larger tug with a smaller engine on a static pull—and then not perform as well with a tow. The reason is obvious: The weight of the larger vessel tends to overcome the surge loads of the tow better than the smaller, more powerful tug. The mass tends to work like a flywheel in sustaining power and compensates for the more modest thrust developed. This is usually more obvious at sea, especially if there is a fair amount of seaway.

TUG PERFORMANCE TABLE

L.O.A.	H.P.	SPEED	HAWSER OR TOW-CABLE SIZE	D.W.T. OF BARGES
1. 72'	500	4 — 6 kts.	600'+ — 6" nylon 600'+ — 7" polypro.	500T — 1,200T
2. 80'	750	5 — 7 kts.	750' — 7" nylon 750' — 8" polypro.	800T — 2,400T
3. 90'	1,000	5 — 7½ kts.	1,000' — 8" nylon	1,000T — 5,000T
4. 100'	1,500	6 — 8½ kts.	1,500' — 8" nylon	1,500T — 9,000T
5. 110'	2,000	6 — 9 kts.	1,500' — 9" nylon	2,500T — 12,000T
6. 115'	3,000	6½ — 8½ kts.	1,800' — 1 3/4" dia. Xtra imp. plow steel	4,000T — 15,000T
7. 120'	4,500	7½ — 9½ kts.	2,200' — 2" dia. Xtra imp. plow steel	5,000T — 20,000T
8. 130'	6,000	7½ — 9½ kts.	3,000' — 2 1/4" dia. Xtra imp. plow steel	8,000T — 35,000T

Another factor is judgment. A fellow tug captain stated it very well, "Sometimes it is more important to have the horsepower in the wheelhouse than in the engine room."

No hard-and-fast rules govern the size of the barge that may be towed in relation to the horsepower of a given tug. There are too many variable factors affecting this, such as overall weather conditions, hull shape of the object to be towed, and experience of the personnel on board the tug.

I have set up a table estimating the size barges that a tug of a given horsepower might be expected to tow offshore. The tonnage given is for the actual deadweight capacity of the vessels rather than the gross tonnage. The table includes an approximate length and size of tow hawsers or cable, as well as the approximate speed of tug and tow in normal moderate weather. Poorly designed barges will not make as much speed for obvious reasons.

The table starts with a tug of 500 h.p. as this is the minimum underwriters will insure over open-water routes.

It must be remembered that a small tug's speed will suffer more than that of a large tug if the weather makes up, and the fuel reserve allotted must be calculated with this in mind.

Chapter 3

The Barge

The origins of the barge are lost in antiquity, but for several thousand years before the steam tug came into existence, men, beasts, wind and current provided the source of energy that bore these vessels and their cargoes to their destinations.

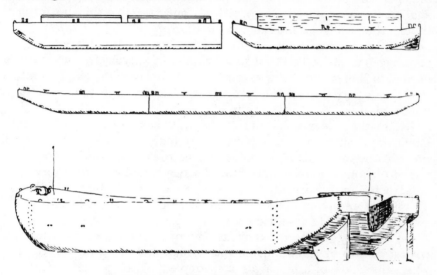

Typical inland and offshore barges.

An Egyptian bas-relief shows how huge stone obelisks were carried on large wooden barges from far up the Nile (above Aswan) to Karnak during the reign of Queen Hapshepsut, more than a thousand years before the Christian era began.

Until recent times the term "barge" was often applied to self-propelled vessels. This would include the "Thames barge" (a sailing vessel) and the self-propelled barges still seen in European waterways. During World War II the term "landing barge" was applied to some of the landing craft used during various invasions in the Pacific and Atlantic areas. The British still use the word "dumb-barge" to denote a barge with no means of propelling itself, either by sail or steam.

A barge is a floating container designed to carry its cargo either inside the hull or on deck. Its simplest form is the scow-shaped deck barge. This is a flat-bottom, slab-sided, square-ended, hull designed to carry all of its cargo on deck. The underbody may be raked at one end, both ends, or may have no rake at all, depending on service. Bulwarks are sometimes added to retain the cargo on board. The scow hull form is by far the most common barge configuration, as it will lift a maximum load for a given length, breadth and depth. It is also the cheapest to construct, and lends itself well to being rafted in with a number of other barges of the same conformation being pushed by a large tugboat.

Some of these craft are fitted with hatches, some with hoppers (both open and closed). There are tank barges for liquid and bulk cargoes, and bottom-opening dump barges designed to dispose of waste from dredging and similar operations. Some have been converted from ships, and others are built with model hulls and resemble ships in form, although the bow is usually much more bluff.

Scow-type barges built for pushing are not likely to have skegs, and may have gusset knees fitted so that units of varying freeboard can be pushed in line without the rake of one sliding over the end of another. Most barges are divided into a number of compartments by watertight bulkheads.

Barges that are pushed and towed will usually have one (and more likely, two) skegs on the after rake. If there are two skegs, they will probably be toed out as this helps to keep the barge from yawing.

For obvious reasons barges built for ocean and coastwise service are constructed more ruggedly than barges used exclusively in inland work. Those that engage in both inland and offshore work will be built to the standards required for outside use.

Occasionally barges are built as part of an integrated tow that may consist of two or three units having sockets and pins which fit together when the ends of the barges are coupled. When properly done this makes a rigid unit. Both end barges will be raked at one end and the middle unit will be square. This makes a sizable tow, but breaks down into easily handled components.

In the past it was the custom to man many barges. Today this practice is not as common due to crew costs and the additional expense of meeting the Bureau of Marine Inspection requirements for manned barges. This is particularly true for barges used in outside service.

Old freighters and windjammers often made a comeback at the end of a towline. In such cases the steering gear was often left intact and a wheel watch maintained while underway. A donkey boiler might be kept to provide a source of power for the anchor windlass and steam heat for the crew.

Pacific Coast lumber companies attempted to dispense with the barge entirely by lashing logs together into a large cigar-shaped bundle to be towed coastwise to the mills. This proved an awkward tow and highly vulnerable to heavy seas and has largely been abandoned except in sheltered waters.

Most sizable ocean-service barges have gone to the model or spoon bow to avoid presenting a large flat area to the sea. Exceptions are barges moving trailer boxes and those designed for lifting large loads of pipe and oil-drilling equipment. Even so, some of these have arced the bottom section forward to ease the pounding.

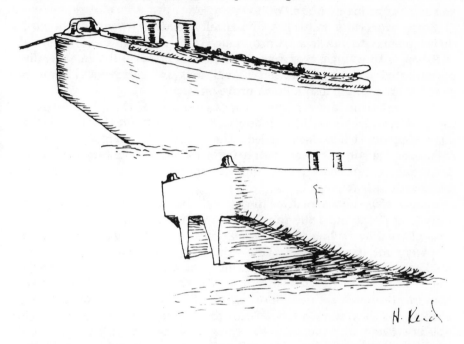

Shown are gusset knees on a barge and bitts on a barge reinforced with cable.

Some large barges have notches in the stern enabling a seagoing tug to push them. When this is done, the area around the notch is reinforced to withstand the thrust from the tug. The practice has proved so successful that a number of towing operations are carried out where the barge is customarily pushed to its destination rather than towed astern, even in boisterous weather. When properly rigged, pushing is feasible without damage in 7' to 8' seas. Needless to say, both are specially fitted to work this way. The tugs are heavily fendered in the area of contact and heavy cables are rigged to hold the tug in position.

Big barges generally have ladders at the bow and stern, and sometimes in the pushing notch, to enable the crew to board the barge when it is light. These hand- and footholds are usually inset on the sides to avoid damage. This is a highly recommended practice for even a modest sized barge. Sending a man up an aluminum ladder in rough conditions is dangerous, but if it is the only way to get on board, it has to be done.

Barges differ greatly in their characteristics. One will tow docilely behind and follow the tug beautifully. Another will just lay to one side or the other of the tug's track, according to the wind direction and force, or perhaps for no discernible reason at all. A really wild barge may not be a cause for alarm at sea, but in confined waters it is nerve-wracking at best. A good set of skegs could prevent a lot of this yawing, but probably not all of it.

Most barges tow well light or partially loaded. When fully loaded their tendency to yaw is most pronounced.

Barges with a single skeg, or two skegs with no toe out, can generally be expected to yaw. Rake-end barges that are narrow and deep in proportion to length also tend to prove erratic.

If the rakes on these narrow barges are short or abrupt, it worsens the performance more. Model bow barges, with good skegs, have the same tendency when deep-loaded. The best towing barges I have encountered are spoon-bowed with a fairly extended rake forward. I cannot recall having seen one with this configuration that towed badly, if fitted with decent skegs.

I once towed two really "disgusting" barges. They were narrow, fairly deep, of about 1800 tons burden, with short rakes and adjustable skegs. I tried every imaginable setting on the skegs to get them to tow properly, but it was useless. One would head one way, and the other would sheer to the opposite side. The short rake ends seemed to cause them to pitch heavily. These were tank barges fitted with fore-and-aft cylindrical containers without baffles. This was done to facilitate cleaning, as they were intended for comestible products. With a high viscosity cargo like molasses these tanks worked properly, but with lighter products that flowed rapidly, the cargo developed enough velocity to blow the hatches off. If there was any free surface at all, the cargo became one big liquid piston. I would watch in amazement as these barges would wallow in a bit of sea and spout their cargo into the air like whales.

A claim for cargo damage was eventually made against the tug. Fortunately I was doing something else on that trip. However, in spite of all the maritime authorities that appeared at the hearing, the real reason for the cargo loss was never raised. It seemed that no one realized that a barge with a characteristic of pitching heavily, fitted with long cylindrical cargo tanks without baffles, might develop pressure too great for the hatch covers to withstand. Perhaps if the hatches were stronger, the tanks may have ruptured. Eventually the action was dropped, but even so, a small amount of the money spent in litigation could have paid the cost of installing baffles, ending the problem of cargo damage. These barges would, of course, still have been difficult to tow.

One thing common to most barges is a general lack of adequate ground tackle. Smaller barges often dispense with anchor, anchor rode, and winch entirely. When barges are fitted with anchor gear it will usually be insufficient or so rusted and corroded as to be useless.

Large barges fortunately seem to be better off in this respect, but most leave a lot to be desired. If port facilities are limited, it may be necessary to nudge the barge onto a mud flat somewhere or jury-rig the tug's anchor so it can be heaved back aboard the tug when the barge is to be shifted. This is one common oversight I would like to see corrected.

Lightly constructed barges being towed without cargo over open water should be ballasted a bit, and perhaps have the forward rake reinforced with timbers. Towing should be at moderate speed during fair weather and even slower during rough, to avoid rupturing the bottom.

If the bitts where the bridles are hooked up look shaky, a couple of turns of cable leading aft to the next set of bitts or cleat and set taut with a turnbuckle will help to distribute the strain.

When picking up a barge to be towed, the captain of the tug should note the draft and assure that the barge is in compliance with loadline regulations, and also check that hatches and watertight doors are properly secured before going to sea.

When a barge is to be moored and left, be sure it is properly secured and will not go adrift. If necessary, provide additional docklines to secure it properly and notify the tug's owners so they can bill for it.

Chapter 4

Gear and Rigging for Coastwise and Ocean Towing

The dictum that "clothes make the man" seems to have fallen on hard times lately. You can be sure, however, that gear and rigging can "make the tugboat."

Regardless of a tug's horsepower, the real limitation on its performance is the amount of strain the various components connecting the tug to its tow can withstand. Gear in poor condition, improperly rigged or poorly matched to the tug's power can oblige an otherwise sound vessel to perform well below its capability. Every piece of gear employed in the "makeup" joining the tug and barge together should be of adequate strength to permit the tug to operate without being hampered by the likelihood of the gear carrying away under the normal range of conditions that one might expect to encounter at sea.

For the sake of simplicity, I have listed the gear more or less in the order of its importance and have then dealt with each item in turn:

1. Tow hawser or tow cable.
2. Bridles, shackles, surge pennants, chafing gear.
3. Supplementary gear: messengers, stoppers, straps, retrieving lines.
4. Working lines and heaving lines.
5. Fender systems and miscellaneous gear.

1. Tow hawsers are usually found in use on tugs where horsepower does not exceed about 2400. This is due simply to the fact that hawsers suitable for greater horsepower are heavy and cumbersome for the small deck force on tugs to handle conveniently. It is more practical to install a towing winch and use a tow cable instead.

The majority of tow hawsers in use today are made from synthetic materials. Nylon is most commonly used. It is excellent and far superior to manila, has tremendous strength and elasticity, and is resistant to chafe and mildew. By reason of its obvious virtues, it is probably the best material of all for use as a tow hawser or for coupling into a tow cable as a shock absorber.

Following nylon in importance would be some of the floating type of hawsers made of polypropylene or a similar material. These hawsers lack the strength and elasticity of nylon and are much more vulnerable to chafe. They can be very handy when used on smaller tugs not fitted with a capstan. At times it is advantageous to use a floating line as an intermediate hawser between the barges in a tandem tow. It is useful, too, when passing a hawser aboard a vessel which is stranded in a reefy area or aground on foul bottom. A normal towline would sink and probably entangle and make hooking-up difficult.

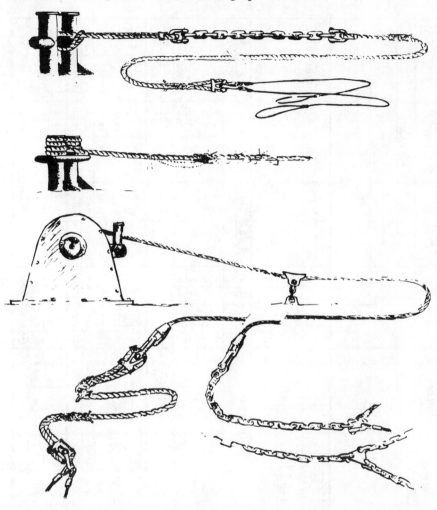

Typical tow hawser and tow cable rigs.

When stowing synthetic hawsers they should be protected against exposure to direct sunlight as this seems to cause deterioration. Avoid having the hawser come in contact with raw gasoline or paint thinners because they tend to dissolve or weaken synthetics.

A hawser must be long and strong enough to do the job. There are no firm rules setting forth the dimensions required for a given tug. However, a rough rule of thumb that seems to work is to allow one foot of

TABLE OF FIBER ROPE STRENGTHS FOR WORKING LINES AND HAWSERS

SIZE		MANILA		POLYPROPYLENE* (Monofilament)		POLY-*plus*		POLY-*cron*		NYLON		DACRON** (Polyester)***	
DIA.	CIR.	Tensile Strength	Lbs. Per 100 Ft.	Tensile Strength	Lbs. Per 100 Ft.	Tensile Strength	Lbs. Per 100 Ft.	Tensile Strength	Lbs. Per 100 Ft.	Tensile Strength	Lbs. Per 100 Ft.	Tensile Strength	Lbs. Per 100 Ft.
3/16"	5/8"	405	1.5	800	.70	—	—	—	—	1,000	1.0	1,000	1.2
1/4"	3/4"	540	2.0	1,250	1.2	—	—	—	—	1,650	1.5	1,650	2.0
5/16"	1"	900	2.9	1,900	1.8	—	—	—	—	2,550	2.5	2,550	3.1
3/8"	1 1/8"	1,215	4.1	2,700	2.8	2,650	3.5	—	—	3,700	3.5	3,700	4.5
7/16"	1 1/4"	1,575	5.25	3,500	3.8	3,600	5.0	—	—	5,000	5.0	5,000	6.2
1/2"	1 1/2"	2,385	7.5	4,200	4.7	4,500	6.5	—	—	6,400	6.5	6,400	8.0
9/16"	1 3/4"	3,105	10.4	5,100	6.1	5,450	7.9	—	—	8,000	8.3	8,000	10.2
5/8"	2"	3,960	13.3	6,200	7.5	6,400	9.4	—	—	10,400	10.5	10,000	13.0
3/4"	2 1/4"	4,860	16.7	8,500	10.7	8,400	12.0	—	—	14,200	14.5	12,500	17.5
13/16"	2 1/2"	5,850	19.5	9,900	12.7	10,200	14.5	—	—	17,000	17.0	15,500	21.0
7/8"	2 3/4"	6,930	22.5	11,500	15.0	12,000	17.0	—	—	20,000	20.0	18,000	25.0
1"	3"	8,100	27.0	14,000	18.0	15,000	21.5	14,000	26.5	25,000	26.0	22,000	30.5
1 1/16"	3 1/4"	9,450	31.3	16,000	20.4	17,100	24.2	—	—	28,800	29.0	25,500	34.5
1 1/8"	3 1/2"	10,800	36.0	18,300	23.7	19,300	27.0	21,000	34.0	33,000	34.0	29,500	40.0
1 1/4"	3 3/4"	12,150	41.8	21,000	27.0	22,000	32.5	24,000	39.0	37,500	40.0	33,200	46.3
1 5/16"	4"	13,500	48.0	23,500	30.5	25,000	38.0	27,000	44.0	43,000	45.0	37,500	52.5
1 1/2"	4 1/2"	16,650	60.0	29,700	38.5	31,300	46.0	34,000	55.0	53,000	55.0	46,800	66.8
1 5/8"	5"	20,250	74.4	36,000	47.5	38,300	55.0	42,000	67.0	65,000	68.0	57,000	82.0
1 3/4"	5 1/2"	23,850	89.5	43,000	57.0	46,500	65.0	50,000	80.0	78,000	83.0	67,800	98.0
2"	6"	27,900	108.0	52,000	69.0	56,500	83.0	60,000	95.0	92,000	95.0	80,000	118.0
2 1/8"	6 1/2"	32,400	125.0	61,000	80.0	65,500	97.0	70,000	112.0	106,000	109.0	92,000	135.0
2 1/4"	7"	36,900	146.0	69,000	92.0	74,000	108.0	80,000	127.0	125,000	129.0	107,000	157.0
2 1/2"	7 1/2"	41,850	167.0	80,000	107.0	86,000	122.0	92,000	147.0	140,000	149.0	122,000	181.0
2 5/8"	8"	46,800	191.0	90,000	120.0	96,000	138.0	105,000	165.0	162,000	168.0	137,000	205.0
2 7/8"	8 1/2"	52,200	215.0	101,000	137.0	105,000	155.0	—	—	180,000	189.0	154,000	230.0
3"	9"	57,600	242.0	114,000	153.0	122,000	179.0	130,000	208.0	200,000	210.0	174,000	258.0
3 1/4"	10"	69,300	299.0	137,000	190.0	144,000	210.0	163,000	253.0	250,000	263.0	210,000	318.0
3 1/2"	11"	81,900	367.0	162,000	232.0	170,000	248.0	—	—	300,000	316.0	254,000	384.0
4"	12"	94,500	436.0	190,000	275.0	200,000	290.0	—	—	360,000	379.0	300,000	460.0

Courtesy of Wall Rope Company

hawser length for each horsepower of propelling force. The hawser should not be less than 600' in length and probably need not be more than 1500'—1800' in length. A hawser's breaking strain should be at least four times the Bollard pull of the tug. When a tug is underway with its tow, the bight of the hawser should lay in the water, except when heavy swells pass.

Though the hawser is strong enough, if its bight keeps coming clear of the surface of the water the hawser is too short and more should be streamed. If not, the speed of the tug and tow will suffer.

As they approach the breaking point, nylon and similar synthetics when placed under heavy strain will vibrate erratically like a cat twitching its tail. When this occurs, power should be reduced immediately and everyone should clear the area.

Splices in synthetic fiber lines require more tucks than those made in manila line. Four tucks will usually hold, but five are better—I have never known a five-tuck splice to fail. For very slippery lines that come under heavy loads, six might be better.

When heaved in on a capstan, regular lay hawser should only be turned in a clockwise direction to prevent kinking the line badly and perhaps damaging it permanently.

As hawsers see service, one end will usually wear more quickly than the other. They should be turned end-for-end at regular intervals in order to get the maximum amount of use from them.

When a thimble is spliced into a tow hawser it should be the heavy-duty type and ought to be solid-welded where the ends come together. There may be a gusset in this area too, for additional strength, and a doubler welded on where the pin of the shackle rides. There are safety thimbles that are better. These are made of heavy malleable cast steel or bronze and have two loops on either side that prevent the thimble from falling out of the eye of the splice. Some tug captains prefer the splice to be up close to the thimble. Others feel that the hawser might stretch enough to allow the thimble to fall out and they prefer to splice in a large eye and seize the thimble in place with a stout lashing. Both systems work well.

Tow cables in use are usually made from extra improved, plow-steel wire rope. They may be six-strand with a hemp core or seven-strand (wire core). To a certain extent the choice depends on the size of the towing winch drum and the strength required of the wire rope. Where the situation permits either option, the six-strand hemp core would probably be the better choice due to the internal lubrications provided. Tow cable is not often galvanized as this adds to the diameter but not the strength.

Tow cables are wound on the towing winch drum which has a level wind device similar to an overgrown fishing reel. Cable is spooled on in even layers. Towing winches may have more than one drum for handling multiple tows. The towing winch may be of automatic or non-automatic type. The difference is that the automatic towing winch will pay out and recover the tow cable at predetermined settings in order to compensate for shockload on the tow cable.

The non-automatic type simply veers or heaves in the cable in response to controls in the hands of an operator.

I prefer the non-automatic type of towing winch, as the ability to pay out and recover is redundant when the gear is properly hooked up and does tend to transfer the shock to the tug.

TOW CABLE STRENGTHS

6 x 19 Class Wire Rope

Rope Diam, in.	Weight per ft, approx lb		*Breaking Strength, tons of 2000 lb			
			Xtra Improved Plow Steel		Improved Plow Steel	
	Fiber Core	IWRC	Fiber Core**	IWRC	Fiber Core	IWRC
1¼	2.63	2.89	71.0	79.9	64.6	69.4
1½	3.78	4.16	101	114	92	98.9
1¾	5.15	5.67	136	153	124	133
2	6.72	7.39	176	198	160	172
2¼	8.51	9.36	220	247	200	215
2½	10.5	11.6	269	302	244	262
2¾	12.7	14.0	321	361	292	314

6 x 37 Class Wire Rope

Rope Diam,	Approx Weight per ft, lb		*Breaking Strengths, tons of 2000 lb			
			Xtra Improved Plow Steel		Improved Plow Steel	
1¼	2.63	2.89	67.7	76.1	61.5	66.1
1½	3.78	4.16	96.6	108	87.9	94.5
1¾	5.15	5.67	130	146	119	128
2	6.77	7.39	169	190	154	165
2¼	8.51	9.36	212	239	193	207
2½	10.5	11.6	260	292	236	254
2¾	12.7	14.0	312	350	284	305

*When ropes are zinc-coated, deduct 10 percent from the bright rope strengths shown.

Courtesy of Bethlehem Steel Co., Wire Rope Division

The inboard end of the tow cable usually passes through a hole in the flange of the winch and is secured in place with a wire clamp. This permits the tow cable to be dropped in an emergency by releasing the brake and spooling out the cable. Some winches, like the surplus stern anchor winch removed from landing ships, still in use on some older tugs, are fitted with a brake that is too lightly constructed to withstand the strain on the tow cable at full power. In such an instance, this deficiency is compensated for by setting up a dog on the drum or another arrangement is made to keep the tow cable from paying out. This can be dangerous if the tow starts to sink in deep water and some provision should be made for cutting the cable to avoid the possibility of the tug being dragged down by its own barge. A complete oxygen-acetylene cutting outfit (with striker and goggles) should be kept at hand for this purpose. I understand that there are explosive-powered cable cutters available. These may be even more effective.

Tow cable terminal fittings may be either an eyesplice, wire rope socket or the new high-pressure swaged fittings. All work well, but the wire rope socket is easier to replace should the outboard end of the cable be damaged and require cropping back. When used in conjunction with the splice or swaged fitting, thimbles should be very strong in order to resist being deformed.

Both tow cable and stern where the cable comes in contact with the taffrail should be heavily greased to protect against wear. The cable should be slacked a bit at regular intervals to distribute the wear as much as possible and prolong its useful life.

2. Bridles are of either chain or wire cable. Chain resists chafe better than cable, but is much heavier and more awkward to work with. It is recommended on long tows where its weight is helpful in absorbing heavy shockloads, and its resistance to chafe provides an additional safety factor. Chain bridles would also be indicated wherever there is a reasonable expectation of encountering ice. Chain bridles are frequently shackled into a fishplate. This is a heavy triangular-shaped steel plate with a reinforced eye at each corner. This is heavy gear and it is common practice to fasten a retrieving line to the fishplate to haul it aboard for connecting or disconnecting.

Some model bow barges dispense with bridles entirely and use a single pennant of wire or chain to make connection.

Under ordinary conditions I prefer wire bridles. They are much easier to handle than chain. The length of bridles is important from the standpoint of convenience. Bridles that are too short require the hawser to be passed aboard the barge to connect up. Bridles that are too long must be heaved clear so that the bight will not foul the propeller when the tug is alongside. If the length of the bridles outboard of the chocks on the barge slightly exceeds the breadth of the barge, it permits the tug to lay alongside and connect up without many gymnastics. A tug can also use the hawser and bridles in lieu of a stern line when the barge is on the hip, saving a little effort in making and breaking tow. The angle made where the bridles join the hawser is only modestly acute and leaves good control over the barge without setting up any great strain on the individual bridle legs.

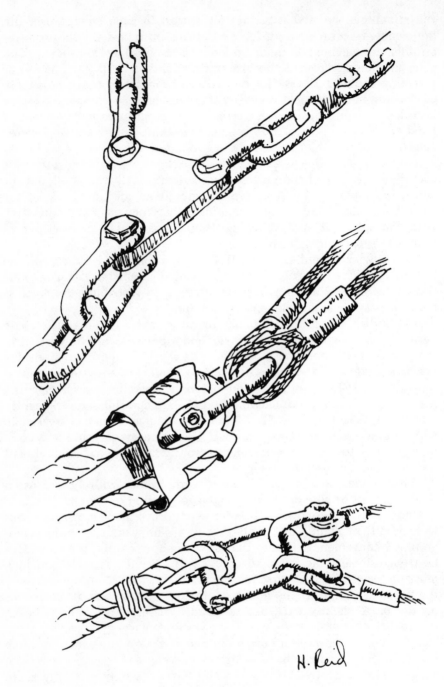

Chain and wire bridles.

The thimble eye in each bridle leg should be large enough to allow the shackle to pass through. This will permit the bridles to ride on the bight of the shackle rather than the pin. If the bridles ride on the pin of a shackle they are likely to deform or break it.

Shackles should be of the approved type. The screw-pin shackle is no longer acceptable to the underwriter and has been replaced by shackles

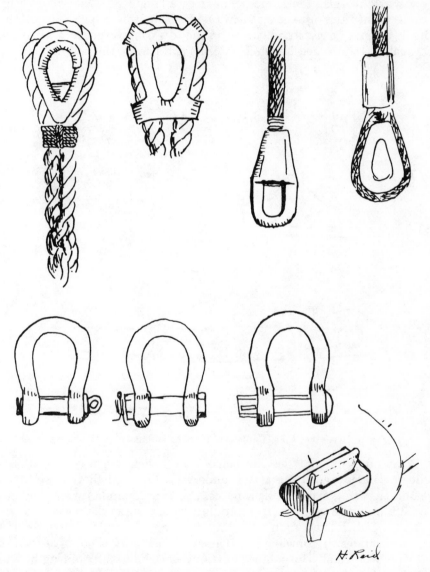

Thimbles and sockets for fiber and cable hawsers: safety shackle, Lowery quick-release shackle, screw-pin shackle.

with a through-bolt type of pin. A heavy cotter key is used to keep the nut from drifting off. There is another approved shackle used for a fast disconnect. This has its pin secured in place by a strong mild steel key like a cotter pin that passes through a slot in the end of the pin and is then doubled over to secure the pin in place.

Tugs that tow with a cable generally shackle the outboard end of the tow wire into a nylon surge pennant or a length of chain which then connects into the bridles. As mentioned before, this helps to absorb the shock when a heavy strain comes on the tow cable, especially when the tow cable is shortened up while entering and leaving the harbor.

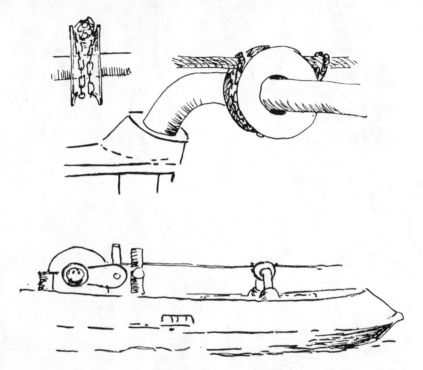

Tug rigged with tow span. Cable is secured to sliding spool to avoid chafe.

A nylon pennant is less nuisance than a chain when coming alongside the barge or getting a tow underway. Provided there is no other reason that would make chain necessary, the better choice would seem to be a nylon shock line. It is certainly easier to handle because of its lighter weight. The length of the nylon pennant would be determined by the dictates of convenience. It might be as short as 60' or as long as 300'. It will usually be somewhere between 150' to 300' in length. The breaking strain of the pennant should approximate that of the cable if possible.

The chain, if used, should be about 90' in length if it can be handled. A shorter length than this may be used, but will not be as effective in absorbing shock loads.

A fiber tow hawser must be protected against chafe. Since it is usually shackled into a bridle or tow pennant where it connects to the barge, there is seldom a problem at the outboard end. If the inboard end makes fast directly to the bitts, the bitts should be wrapped with canvas or burlap. This is especially important where the first turn comes off the bitts. The hawser must also be protected where it comes in contact with the taffrail. This is usually done by lashing a towing board

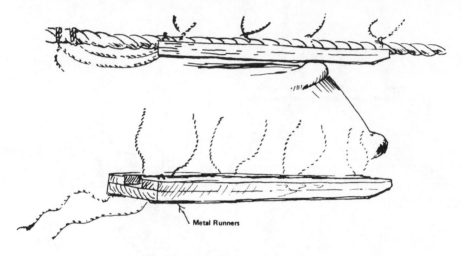

Metal Runners

Towing board arrangement.

to the hawser at this point, or shackling the tow hawser into a length of anchor chain that extends outboard of the stern of the tug. This length of chain is in turn shackled into a fiber strap that is made fast to the bitts. The fiber strap permits the tow to be released in an emergency, as it can be severed with an axe. The strap is often made up from a doubled piece of the same material as the hawser. The stern should be greased where the chain rubs across it to minimize wear on the chain as well as the rail.

When the tow hawser is connected to the bitts by a chain and strap in this fashion it is quite trouble-free. It may be a little more laborious to shorten up than a hawser fitted with a towing board, but it eliminates the problem of the towing board capsizing, which is a frequent occurrence. Should this happen, the hawser can chafe through in a short time if a sharp watch is not maintained.

3. Tugs require certain items of equipment in addition to the gear employed in linking together the tug and its tow. This equipment is

employed to assist the crew in making and breaking tow, as well as shortening up a hawser prior to entering a harbor.

One of the most important pieces of line is the messenger which is usually manila, but synthetic fiber lines work quite well. This will normally be between 100' and 150' in length and will probably have a heavy hook spliced into one end. This messenger is used for leading to the capstan whenever bridles or perhaps a chafing chain have to be heaved aboard, or when the tow hawser must be heaved up for shortening the tow.

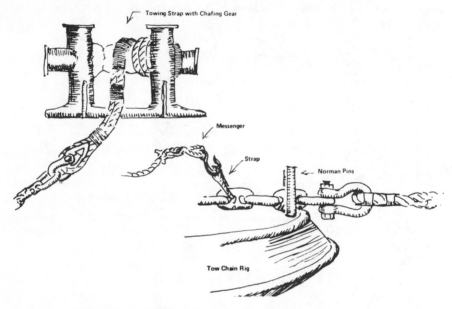

Illustration of towing strap and Norman pin arrangement.

Along with the messenger, the tug should be provided with sufficient stoppers, 2 or 3 fathoms long, and chain stoppers if the tug uses a tow cable. Small straps, 18" or 20" long with an eye at both ends are very useful for passing around hawser chains, bridles and hooking the eye into the messenger.

Retrieving lines are lengths of line that serve the same purpose as the messenger, but are usually attached permanently to the bridles on the barge. Floating synthetic lines like polypropylene work well for this and should be a little stronger than the messenger for day-to-day use. The amount of retrieving line that is out when the bridles are fully stretched should be marked so that the strain of the tow hawser will not be brought directly to bear on it when it is secured in place on the barge while underway.

4. In addition to the gear actually needed for making and breaking the tow, the tug must have other working lines. These lines are for making the tug fast alongside the barge when it is maneuvering in the harbor. While nylon line is wonderful for a tow hawser, it is much too elastic for this work. Dacron and some other synthetic fiber lines are much better. None are as strong as nylon, but they do not stretch as much, either. Working lines should be about 150' in length with an eye splice at one or both ends—according to the needs. In some trades where tugs are handling the same barges all the time, the spring line may be made up to the correct length and made fast by dropping the eyes over the appropriate bitts. These are sometimes referred to as "towing straps."

Heaving lines should be kept on hand, fore and aft, on a tug. At times short heaving lines are very handy for passing working hawsers up onto a light barge; 3/8" manila is a good size for heaving lines as it offers a good handhold. The tug should also be equipped with regular heaving lines, 15 or 20 fathoms in length.

5. A few years ago deck crews on tugs spent a lot of time making and mending bow fenders. The fenders were usually made from worn-out manila hawser saved for this purpose. Today rubber bow fenders have come into use and crew wages are so high it is probably more economical to buy fenders than it would be to make them. Manila is not plentiful and the synthetics (regardless of their other virtues) do not lend themselves to this purpose very well. Old truck and tractor tire casings are effective side fenders, either in their original state or cut into squares and strung on heavy steel rods. Sometimes bow fenders are made this way from laminates of discarded truck tire cases. The real advantage of the rope fender over the rubber one is the traction it provides when working alongside a slippery ship hull with a single-screw tug. I have assisted some tankers that had picked up a light film of oil on their freeboard and a single-screw tug would skid up and down the side while trying to get in position with a rubber bow fender whereas a tug with the old rope fenders could work well without sliding very much.

Aluminum ladders are fairly standard gear for getting the mate and deckhands up on a light barge. They should have light lines spliced around the shafts at appropriate places so they can be made fast temporarily. When they get damaged (which is inevitable), they should be discarded and replaced.

Spare hawsers are usually discarded hawsers that have seen enough service. If they are badly worn, do not temporize. They should not even be used as spares, but turned into dock lines for the barge or kept as an anchor rode should the tug be required to anchor in foul bottom.

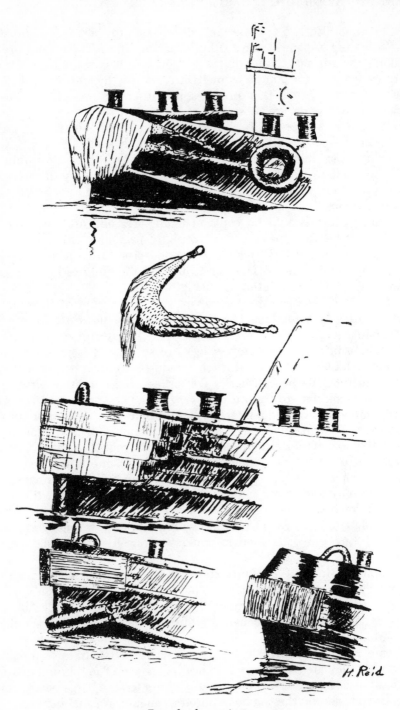

Bow fender systems.

Many tugs working outside have a set of Norman pins in the stern. This is a type of chock that keeps the hawser or tow cable in the center of the stern. It does make steering much easier. Sometimes the pins may be hydraulically operated or may be simply a set of steel bars that fit into vertical openings near the taffrail on either side of the center line.

Tugs with cluttered afterdecks often have a strongback tow span across from one side to the other to keep the hawser or cable from fouling on obstructions. Occasionally the tow span will have a traveling metal spool in which the tow cable fits to protect it from wear at this spot.

A gob line may be fitted to keep the hawser or tow cable from jumping out of the pins when the tug is pitching heavily in a sea. This may be a simple lashing fitted to a pad eye, conveniently located in the afterdeck, or may be a fitting specifically designed for this purpose.

All of the above gear, when properly rigged and accompanied by common sense and experience, assures that the tug will perform its appointed tasks with ease and efficiency.

Chapter 5

Ship Work

Ship work, harbor service, or transportation are some of the terms used to designate the employment of a tug or number of tugs when assisting a larger vessel to dock or undock. Tugs are often called upon to provide assistance to ships passing through locks and bridges, and transiting narrow waterways.

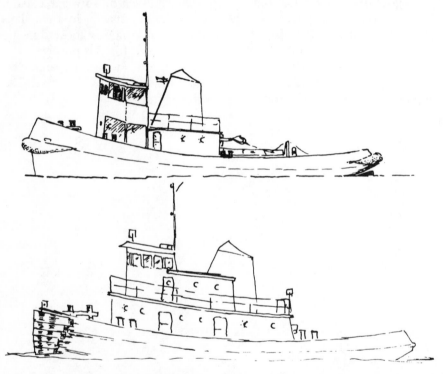

Examples of European and American harbor tugs.

The tug is generally acting in response to orders from the ship's master or pilot. However, it is not uncommon in some areas for the towing company supplying the tugs to provide the services of a docking master who will usually give directions to his own tug and any others being used.

Methods of employing the tugs vary widely in different areas. For example, European tugs ordinarily work with a short towline, and seldom go alongside a ship. Such tugs usually have a tow hook to which the eye of the towline is secured. This permits the hawser to be released by tripping the hook in the event that the tug is caught in a situation that threatens to capsize it. The tow hook is generally located further forward than the bitts on American tugs. This permits a great deal of maneuverability. Many European tugs have bridge wings to permit greater visibility aft, and if they do go alongside of a ship it must be in an area where there is little or no flare, or else approach bows-on to avoid damaging them.

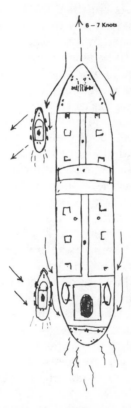

Tugs coming alongside an inbound ship. Diagonal arrows indicate common hydraulic effect on the tugs at bow and near the stern.

American tugs, on the other hand, often make fast alongside the vessel especially when the ship is inbound, and will either push or back as required by the situation. For this reason they normally have fairly narrow wheelhouses and often the mast can be lowered. This helps to prevent damage to the tug when working close to the bow or stern of the ship where the flare and overhang are greatest.

Tugs that work alongside ships should be heavily fendered to protect them and the ships from damage. The bow fender in particular should be large enough and sufficiently rugged to cushion the force of the tug's thrust and distribute it over a wide area so that injury to the ship is avoided.

When an inbound ship is being docked, the tugs will usually make fast on the side of the ship that will be outboard when the ship is berthed. They will assist the ship to steer while approaching the dock, and then breast her in against the wind and tide, or hold her off as is necessary while the ship gets out the docklines.

When a ship is undocked the tug or tugs are used to help maneuver the ship clear of its berth and into the stream, and then assist the vessel to turn if necessary for it to be able to proceed safely to its destination. This maneuver may require one or more tugs, and common logic should govern the method of employing them.

Barge work and other phases of towboating require as much "savvy" as ship work, but ship work is more hazardous. The underlying cause of this often may be laid to a lack of understanding, or faulty communication between the ship and tug. For this reason, good communication between the tug and ship is of vital importance, and the pilot and tug operators should be in complete rapport. VHF communication should be used whenever possible. Whistle signals should be understood by all concerned, but employed only when the necessity arises, or for the tug to acknowledge the pilot's order.

Some pilots, in spite of being excellent shiphandlers, have little conception of the problems that confront a tug's captain performing a harbor service, and may direct him to place the tug in a position that is dangerous. If the tug's captain objects, the pilot might find it difficult to understand his reasons. When this happens, the tug captain should be firm and polite, and try to explain why it is inadvisable to place the tug in that situation. It usually helps to point out that the ship may also be damaged. A pilot or ship captain may be indifferent about banging up the tug, but they are usually reluctant to embark on a course of action that might damage the ship.

Methods of employing a tug in ship work vary a great deal. There are usually two or three alternate ways of using the tugs in a given situation to accomplish the same purpose. Different pilots use different methods. Any tug operator undertaking to assist a vessel should acquaint himself with that particular pilot's intentions. Misunderstandings often lead to damage and are apt to cause ill feelings between the pilot and the crew on the tug.

The young man breaking in as mate on a tug will probably discover the most difficult part of harbor service is putting the tug alongside an inbound ship that is moving at a good rate of speed. If he is careless and tries to accelerate the maneuver, he is likely to hit the ship too hard and do some damage.

When a tug is going alongside a moving vessel it is a good idea to shape a course more or less parallel for a little bit, and adjust the speed to that of the vessel. Then ease the tug in gently and compensate for the effect of the vessel's wash.

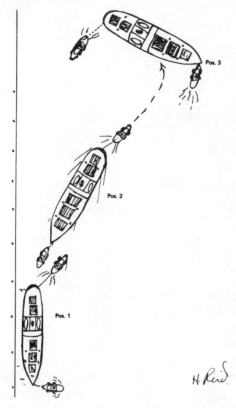

Two tugs assisting a ship to unberth.

When a tug intends to go alongside the ship on the after quarter, the suction at the stern will have a tendency to pull the tug in to the vessel. Usually, pacing it with the helm turned slightly away from the ship will utilize the suction to an advantage to pull the tug in easily. As soon as the tug comes against the ship, the helm should be put over towards the ship and the engine kept running ahead to keep the tug alongside until the lines are fast. Ideally, the tug should land against the ship about its own midships or a bit aft of that, and then swing the bow in gently as the helm is put over toward the ship.

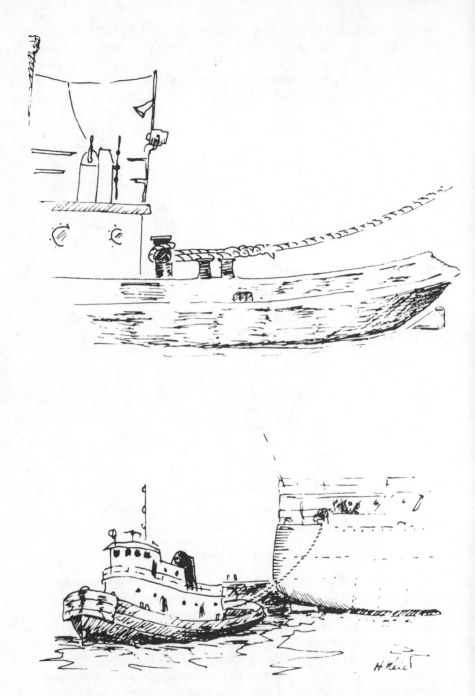

(Top) A typical after control station on a harbor tug. (Bottom) A tug with tow-line up, preparing to assist a ship.

While it is generally less hazardous to come alongside a ship forward, it still requires care. The tug is more likely to be pushed away by the bow wave, especially if the vessel's entrance is hollow or if it is sponsoned out like some of the container ships. The problem here is usually one of over-controlling while coming alongside. Pacing the ship, however, will usually solve this problem.

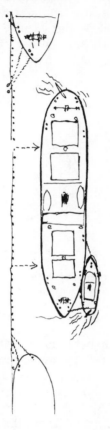

Tug made up on bow of ship. Tug's engine half ahead; ship engine dead slow ahead. Both ship and tug have their wheels turned hard over towards the dock. Vessel will move sidewise away from berth.

Working on a towline in harbor service is probably the most dangerous employment that a tug will normally engage in. This is especially so if the pilot or master is excitable or relies too heavily on the use of the ship's engine.

When working on a towline, a tug operator will normally be at the after control station where he can keep an eye on the deck force and on the ship's wheelwash. The wheelwash will often give a clue as to the amount of power the ship's engine is using, and the tug can be maneuvered to compensate for this. The tug's hawser should be leading toward a vessel's anticipated direction of movement. If it seems that the ship will move ahead or astern rapidly, the tug should attempt to get parallel to avoid a capsizing situation. If this is not possible, the tug should stop engines and put the helm midships. The tug will probably be dragged stern-first by the ship (and may do some damage if it strikes the ship) but this is preferable to being rolled over.

If the ship is stopped dead in the water, or moving slowly, there will be no problems and the tug can be used to best effect. Towline length

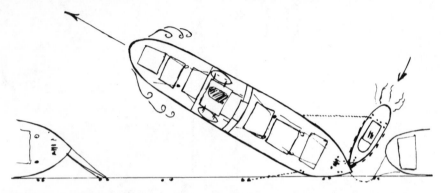

Tug with bowline and quarter line up assisting freighter to undock. Tug first breasts freighter's bow in to open the stern and then will back or push as necessary to steer the freighter as it backs out of its berth. Quarter line will keep the tug in position during this maneuver.

for this operation should be between 100' and 150', conditions permitting. Insist on using a non-elastic hawser for working lines employed in harbor service. A parting nylon line can be murderous.

Special care must be taken when shifting the controls from pilothouse to after station. Many accidents happen as a result of someone "playing" with the after control without the skipper's knowledge.

If a service is pending that will be a towline job, the after control station should be uncovered before the tug leaves the dock, and checked to see that things are as they ought to be. The axe should be readily available in case it becomes necessary to sever the hawser. A hawser or working line should never be slacked when under heavy strain, and the deckhands should be so advised.

The diagrams on accompanying pages show a number of situations that a tug doing ship work might expect to encounter. There is no doubt that there are many others, but common sense and experience will usually provide the answer regarding the best application of the tug's power and maneuverability to aid the ship.

There are a number of "Do's and Don'ts" that should be brought to the novice tug operator's attention that may help to avoid some bruises and lumps, especially to the new operator's self-esteem. Unfortunately, like any advice, these do not substitute for experience:

1) Do not back full astern on a slack headline; you may part it. Go astern easily until it comes tight, and then gradually increase the power.

2) When an order is received to stop backing, drop power to slow astern and then stop the engine. But be ready to check the tug's headway if it is propelled too rapidly toward the ship by the elasticity of the hawser.

Tug making fast to a Panama or pocket chock in the side of a passenger liner. Note how line is passed through chock and bitter end is made fast back aboard tug.

3) When assisting ships (usually passenger liners) that have Panama or pocket chocks located low down on the freeboard, have a line ready that is small enough in diameter to pass through them. This line should have an eye only at one end, and a good whipping at the other so that it will pass through freely. This line can be smaller than the regular working line as it will be doubled.

4) Never let the tug get positioned between the ship and the dock when coming in. This makes "long skinny tugboats." Stay in position as long as you can and then notify the pilot of the situation and remove

the tug. Do not wait too long to do so, because the tug may be washed in if the ship backs hard.

5) When coming alongside a ship underway, the operator should not allow himself to be distracted. This entire maneuver is an exercise in relative movement and a little carelessness or lack of attention can have disheartening results.

6) When whistle signals are used, the bow tug will normally respond to the pilot's mouth whistle, and the tugs aft to the ship's whistle. Basic signals are:

One blast	— Full ahead
One blast	— Stop
Two blasts	— Full astern
One long + two short	— Tug is released or is to change positions

There are local variations to be encountered, and the newcomer should familiarize himself with them. Also, beware of echoes off high buildings close to the dock, and the possibility of a traffic cop on a nearby street blowing his whistle while directing traffic. Should you encounter difficulty in hearing signals, have the mate on the bow or stern relay the orders to you.

7) When a ship is going to back out of the berth stern-first, it is sometimes convenient for the bow tug to work against the stem. If you do not have a line up (so that the ship knows you are there) be sure to give a toot on the whistle and remind the mate not to dump the anchor on top of the tug.

8) When coming alongside a ship, the tug's crew should not attempt to pass the hawser aboard until the tug is in position, pressed against the ship's side. If this is not done, should the tug take a sheer away from the ship, a long length of working hawser may fall into the water. At best it will be a difficult task to recover it, and the tug will probably have to stop to permit this. The possibility also exists that the line might be lost, foul the tug's or ship's wheel, or injure the seaman as it pays out.

9) A twin-screw tug, when making fast alongside a ship will usually only have to put up a single headline. However, on a ship with badly placed chocks, a single-screw tug may require two lines—a headline and springline—to work safely. Lead the springline from the bow aft to enable the tug to pivot on it freely. The headline or line leading forward can make fast elsewhere as it will be needed for backing down only.

10) When backing a ship off the dock, a single-screw tug may use a quarter line in addition to the headline. This line leads from the quarter bitts aft and helps the tug remain in position by countering the effect of torque which will drift the stern to port on a normal right-hand turning engine.

11) Diesel electric tugs are popular for harbor work as they provide

a wide range of speeds, and the tug can stay in position without pressing heavily on the ship. Tugs with controllable-pitch wheels must handle the lines carefully since the propellers never stop turning. They have earned a reputation as "hawser suckers" for this reason.

12) Tugs doing a lot of towline work may be fitted with a tow hook. A short strap may be utilized to the same effect. The eye is dropped over the tow bitt, the bight passes through the eye of the ship's hawser, and the bitter end made fast to the bitts. A deckhand can usually slack this away without danger to himself should it be necessary to let go the ship's hawser.

A method of making a headline fast when there is an upward lead. This prevents the line from coming adrift.

13) Working lines on harbor tugs fray rapidly. Replacement should be made when they begin to show much wear. Some harbor tugs use a wire pennant at the outboard end to avoid chafe. I personally do not care for this, as the cable soon develops "fishhooks" and big ship crews have a nasty habit of letting the tug's line go on the run. I would rather be hit by a hawser than a heavy cable pennant full of broken wires. A hawser is also easier to recover if it falls in the water.

14) Some tugs are fitted with a closed bow chock called a "bull-nose." This is preferable to having only a bitt forward for taking on the first turns. The size of the opening should be large enough to pass the eye and splice of working hawser with ease.

15) When a tug is working alongside the quarter of a light ship, be sure the watertight doors and ports are closed on the inboard sides to prevent the tug from being flooded by overboard discharges from the ship.

16) Care must be taken when a tug crosses a ship's wake. The turbulence will frequently cause the tug's propeller to cavitate. If the tug is

approaching a ship under this circumstance with too much speed, it may collide with the vessel as the tug's propeller might not have the desired effect when the tug's engines are backed down in order to stop the tug.

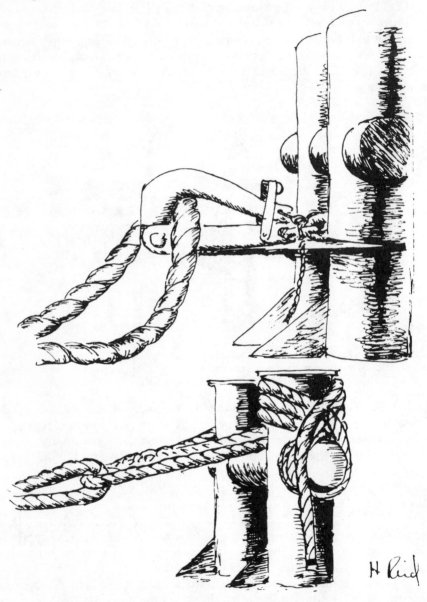

Illustration shows tow hook and alternate method of using a strap for tow-line jobs.

Chapter 6

Barge Handling

Tugs often engage in moving barges, lighters, dead ships and miscellaneous vessels about the harbor. This will involve docking, undocking and maneuvering to convey the charge to its destination. The technique used usually consists of pushing, towing, or moving with the barge fast alongside the tug. This is referred to as having the barge "on the hip." Since pushing is explained in Chapter 9 (Inland and River Towing), we will deal here with towing and on-the-hip maneuvering.

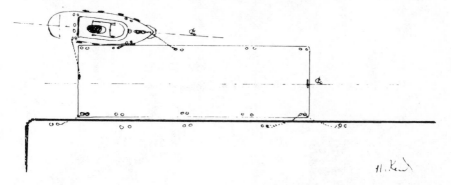

Tug with barge "on the hip." Note inclination of center line of tug in relationship to center line of barge.

When moving a barge "on the hip," a tug will usually make fast alongside where it is most convenient, either at the bow or stern of the barge. Factors such as ease of docking or undocking, or the need to have a certain end of the barge inboard at a given berth, will determine the position.

The tug's stern should be back far enough to have good steerage and will usually employ at least three lines to make fast, a headline, a spring- and a sternline. When a tug handles the same size barge often enough, a springline may be made up to the length required with an eye spliced at each end. This enables the deckhand to drop the eye over the appropriate bitts without having to make the inboard end fast in the normal fashion. The line is then referred to as a "tow strap." When the bitts on the barge do not conform to those on the tug, the lead of the headline and springline may be reversed. This works fairly well, but the conventional method of lashing up is preferred.

When the tug is properly made fast, there should be a minimum

41

amount of slack in the lines so the tug's operator will have maximum
control over the barge. To accomplish this the tug will put out a springline first and then work ahead on its engine with the wheel turned
toward the barge. The headline is then put out. When the headline is

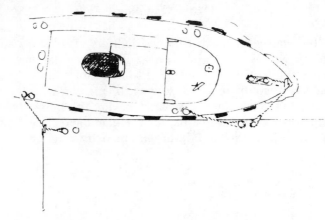

Alternate arrangement for making barge fast on the hip.

Methods of making lines fast; turns taken clockwise when possible.

made fast the wheel is turned away to swing the stern of the tug in
toward the barge. This results in the headline coming tight. The sternline is then made fast or perhaps even heaved a bit on the capstan.

When the tug is secured in place, the center line of the tug should lay
at a slight inclination, bow in, to the center line of the barge. When the
tug's angle is too great, either in or out, the barge is awkward and
sometimes impossible to control. Should the barge be light and much
higher than the tug, take care to make the lines fast in a way that will
prevent them from coming adrift. Most quarter bitts (both fore and aft)

are fitted with horns for this purpose. The common method used is to put a half hitch around the bitt and then pass a turn beneath the horn and make fast as usual. It is sometimes wise to lead the sternline from the far side of the barge or across the stern of the tug, because if the lead is up and down, the stern of the tug will be free to move about and control over the barge will suffer.

Once the tug is properly made up to the barge it can maneuver as required to clear the berth. This may require "springing" the barge open, either ahead or astern. When the barge is clear of its berth it can proceed to its destination.

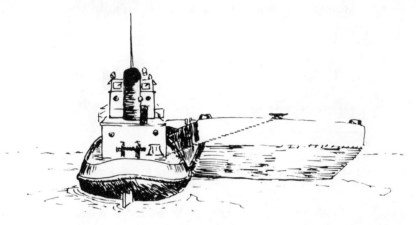

Tug with light barge on hip. Note tug's sternline is led across barge for better lead.

A few things should be called to the attention of anyone not familiar with handling a barge "on the hip." For one thing, the operator is obliged to pick a spot on the barge to steer by. With a conventional ship the bow is pointed in the desired direction, making only a small correction for drift if it is necessary. With barges this is usually not the case. They are for the most part, flat bottomed and tend to drift a great deal in fresh winds, especially when light. The operator will often be required to compensate for this tendency by steering a course that varies considerably from the course made good. Barges also "crab" sideways if the tug is required to use large angles of helm to steer the barge. The effect tends to cause the whole rig to slide in the opposite direction from that of the helm.

It takes practice to adjust to this, and until the operator has acquired enough experience to do so (more or less automatically), he should pay close attention to whatever ranges are available.

When docking a barge "on the hip" the tug is usually on the outboard side from the dock. When the tug starts to back its engine and the "bow" of the barge (or whichever end of it happens to be forward at the time) will usually swing away from the dock. A light barge will usually swing more than a heavily loaded one and the approach should be a little steeper. Keep an eye on the wind as this can change things.

A barge's characteristic of turning toward the side the tug is on when the tug backs is useful in steering, especially when making an approach to the dock. You can steer the barge by using the engine, giving a touch astern or ahead as is needed to keep it straight while continuing to make a slow approach without getting too much headway on the barge.

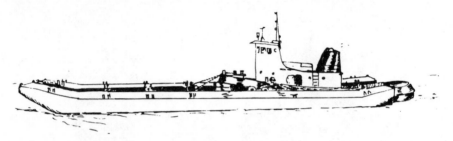

Tug handling two barges "on the hip." Bows of barges secured together.

A tug operator is often completely dependent on the man on the barge giving signals. This is especially so if the barge is sizable and light in draft preventing the operator from seeing the dock. Tug captains often stand on the barge and give orders to the mate at the controls while docking. But often the tug captain will have to depend on the deckhands for signals while docking and undocking. If this is the case, make sure that an inexperienced hand gets plenty of practice until he becomes proficient. It is best to have a seasoned hand stand by until the new man becomes adept. Hand signals used should be demonstrated to him, and since he will usually be posted forward, instructions should be given to look aft from time to time in order to be able to judge the barge's swing.

While a tug captain may be an accomplished handler, unless he has taken pains to insure that the one directing the maneuver from the barge is well practiced and skillful, the whole maneuver may be botched.

A tug may hip two or more barges at the same time. When a tug has a barge on each side, the "makeup" is the same as is used for handling one barge, but the forward ends of the barges should be lashed together.

In passing, it is worth noting that in some areas barges are shifted about using only a "tow strap" or springline. The tug crew will usually drop a line over a bitt or a cleat nearly midship on the barge and make it fast on the tug's forward quarter bitts. A skilled handler can shift a lot of barges in a short time in this manner, but it is rougher on the barges because one line simply will not give the same degree of control over a barge as three lines properly placed and secured.

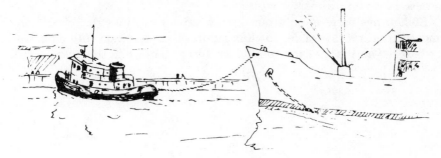

Tug berthing a dead ship on a towline. Ship has one shackle of chain in the water.

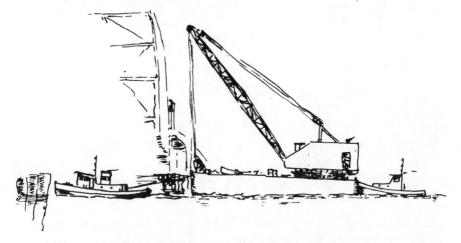

Tug and tail boat handling derrick barge.

Often it is practical for the tug to handle a barge "on the string" or short towline. If the barge has a short rake, is square-ended, or deep-loaded so that the after rake will not slide over the stern, a tug with a well fendered stern can often steam into a berth slowly and check the barge's way by backing down against the barge's bow. This works well, but must be done at slow speed.

A tug can handle a much larger barge on a towline than it can "on the hip." This is especially so if the barge is light and there is a bit of wind blowing. In a case when a dead ship or large barge is being handled, two tugs are often used—one towing the ship, and the other one fast on the stern with either a single headline up or two of them rigged as a bridle. The tug on the stern can check the headway by backing and will also be able to steer the vessel a bit by putting its own rudder over hard and sheering the stern to one side or other. Two tugs working in conjunction this way are usually able to control the barge as much as is necessary under ordinary conditions.

Sometimes there is only one tug available, but if conditions of wind and current are favorable, towline landings can be made with a big ship or barge. The anchor can often be used to advantage in this case. A shot

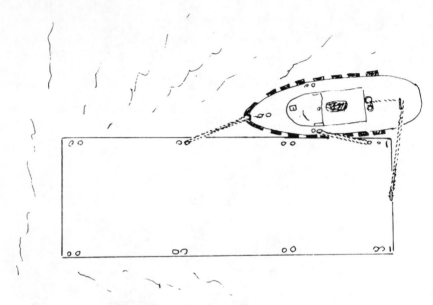

Tug with extra heavy fenders and working lines doubled on long leads
for working barge alongside in exposed area.

of chain in the water is usually sufficient if the tug is towing very slowly. Sometimes it is worthwhile to drop the anchor and then tow the ship, or barge, stern-first into the berth. Just make sure that no cable areas are crossed in the process of doing so.

When handling a barge on a towline through curving channels, the barge will tend to go at first in the opposite direction of the tug's turn. This characteristic can be helpful when used with discretion, for should the operator find the barge setting down too much onto a buoy, it might be better to turn the tug toward the buoy and apply more power. This will often swing the barge away from the buoy, and when the barge is clear the tug can straighten out again. This works better with a light barge than a loaded one. Care should be taken with a large, deeply laden barge or dead ship on a towline, and sharp bends should be negotiated at slow speed to avoid having the tug overpowered by the weight of the tow.

When leaving a dock it is sometimes convenient to take a barge out on a towline. This should be done at slow speed. Barges usually have to swing a bit, and if power is applied rashly it can cause damage by accelerating the barge's swing one way or the other. Patience and moderation avoid a lot of unnecessary damage.

Barges are not usually handled on the hip "outside," but in oil field work this is often necessary. Damage should be expected. To minimize this, working lines should have long leads and be doubled. The tug should be fendered as much as possible. Even a slight swell causes a certain amount of surging and must be expected. Tug personnel should exercise extra caution to avoid injury. The barge should also be fendered if it has to lay alongside other vessels.

Barge handling is one of the staple employments of tugs, and the skill required to do it well is often taken for granted. But for the knowledgeable onlooker, it can be a treat to see an able handler practice his art.

Chapter 7

Making and Breaking Tow

When a tug is getting underway with a tow, it will go alongside the bow of the barge if possible, and put up a springline and a headline. The hawser will then be connected to the bridles on the barge. If the bridles on the barge are the right length, the towline and bridle can be heaved tight and made fast and used as the sternline.

Tug with barge on hip ready to stream tow.

The tug can then maneuver clear of the dock and proceed to where the barge can be dropped astern on a short hawser. If it is gusty and the barge is light, the tug should maneuver so the wind will hold the barge against the tug to enable personnel to get off easily. It is best to be stopped in the water before casting off the headline and spring.

When these are cast off the tug can come ahead easily, turning away from the barge and veering hawser until a proper length has been reached. The tug can then proceed out the channel to sea with the barge on a short hawser. Once outside and clear of traffic, the rest of the hawser or tow cable is veered and the tug can proceed on its voyage.

Often all of this is not necessary and many times the barge is laying in such position that it is possible to hook up the hawser to the barge, cast off the barge dockline, and sail directly from the berth with the barge on a short towline. This should be done at slow speed for as the barge gets underway it is almost certain to swing a certain amount. It will also swing back as well, and if too much power is given it might overswing and do some damage.

Coming into port is basically a reverse of the operation of sailing. The tug arrives off the harbor entrance and starts shortening hawser in an area clear of traffic. The bottom here should be clear of obstacles or the water deep enough to keep the hawser from fouling on the bottom. If the tug has a towing winch it can usually heave in its tow wire while moving slowly ahead.

This operation is more involved on a hawser tug. The tug should slow down and get most of the way off the barge. When both units are pretty well slowed down, the hawser is stopped off and led to the capstan. This may require using a messenger to pull in the chain, and enough slack in the hawser to make sufficient turns about the capstan. Once the hawser is on the capstan, the tug can maneuver a bit to keep the towline clear until the hawser is short enough to enter the harbor.

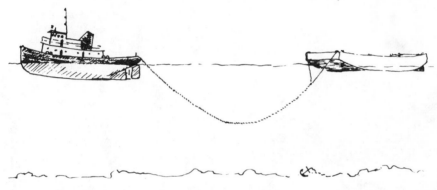

Tug shortening hawser before entering harbor. Note reason for keeping hawser clear of bottom.

As mentioned before, regular lay three-strand tow hawser should only be heaved in in a clockwise direction. This avoids kinks in the line that might permanently ruin it. When the hawser is coming in it should be coiled or faked free for running the next time. This takes longer, but saves a lot of grief later on.

During the process of shortening up, the tug should try to keep the hawser leading away from the propeller over one quarter or the other. Having the faster drifting vessel to leeward at the start may save some maneuvering to keep the towline clear. When shortening up at night, a good searchlight is essential to illuminate the hawser and the barge and to avoid entangling the hawser in the propeller.

The hawser should be shortened enough to permit good control over the barge, usually between 100' to 300' depending on circumstances. The Coast Guard restricts hawser length to 450' under normal conditions.

If the tug has to cross a bar and sea conditions are heavy, it may require more hawser length than this. In this case, the tug captain should determine that the channel is clear before proceeding in.

Once the tug and tow are inside, the tug must maneuver to berth its charge. If it is a large barge or a ship, and there is an assisting tug, it might towline it right alongside the dock and berth it in this fashion. Normally the tug will "hip up" to the barge and berth it. There are a lot of tricks of the trade in this maneuver and a lot of good shiphandlers have had their spirits dampened while undertaking to come alongside a barge for the first time.

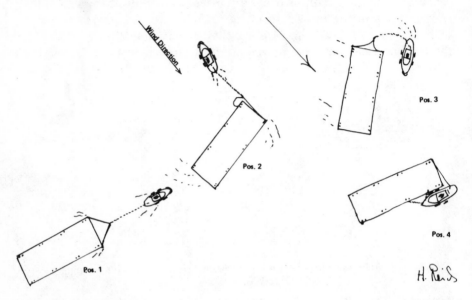

Tug making fast alongside a light barge. Notice that the tug goes to the lee to use the wind to best effect.

The tug will usually try to use the wind to advantage. For example, trying to catch a light barge on a windy day, from the weather side, can be a frustrating process. An experienced tug skipper will check the barge's way by giving it a short turn, and then maneuver the tug to leeward of the barge. The wind will then blow the barge right alongside, and hold it there while the lines are made up.

Unless a tug has a tailboat assisting, about the only way a tug can check the speed of a barge (other than wait for it to slow down of its own accord) is to turn it. That is, the tug maneuvers over to one side without putting a strain on the hawser, and when the barge is astern of the tug and their tracks more or less at 90° to each other, the tug comes ahead and starts the barge turning. The barge will spin off a lot of its energy and may stop completely.

If the barge is big and loaded it will carry way for unbelievable distances. It may overpower the tug if the tug tries to turn it sharply and drag the tug alongside sternforemost. Some skippers use the forward motion of the barge to assist them in making up alongside. But, beware the hawser. A sharp eye must be kept on how the hawser leads, for if it is allowed to pass under the tug it can foul the wheel. It might also lead to a capsize if there is a large, fast-moving barge on the other end of it. Until one is practiced at making up to a barge, the best thing is to go slow and let the barge get most of its way off before attempting to maneuver alongside.

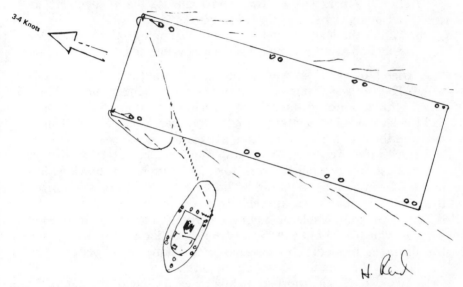

Danger! The tug has allowed the hawser to pass beneath it. It may foul the propeller or capsize the tug.

Avoid working with the hawser too short for the tug to maneuver. This can lead to a situation where the barge is chasing the tug around in circles. Also, the tug should keep clear of the barge's rake end, particularly if the barge is light. Too short a hawser has caused a lot of damage as a result of this type of contact.

When a good tug captain makes up to a barge it may look like a lot of aimless maneuvering to the uninitiated. But many times he will come out of the maneuver all made up and headed in the right direction to berth the barge.

This reminds me of watching a good professional boxer loaf through a round, flurry for the last ten or fifteen seconds to make points, and be in his own corner when the bell is rung and he can sit down and rest. Salient points to remember are:

1. Veer and shorten up the hawser in areas clear of marine traffic.
2. Be sure there is enough water under you to avoid fouling the hawser on the bottom.
3. Keep the hawser clear of the wheel.
4. Heave regular lay fiber hawser clockwise.
5. Do not shorten hawser too much if the bar is rough.
6. Check traffic in channel outbound if the hawser is long due to sea conditions.
7. Let the barge slow down and then use the elements to an advantage when making up alongside.
8. Watch the lead of the hawser when spinning a barge to reduce way and avoid getting caught under rake ends.

A friend of mine is captain of a tug towing a 100,000-barrel oil barge. The tug was formerly used for anchor-running in the Gulf, and is fitted with a double-drum towing winch. One drum of the winch has had the level wind apparatus removed, and there is just a short length of cable on the drum. The other drum is rigged in the conventional fashion and carries the tow cable. This drum, of course, has a level wind device.

When he is preparing to break tow, he shortens up the cable in the normal fashion, and enters the harbor. He can then heave in all of his tow cable and disconnect the cable from the nylon shockline. When this is done, the short cable on the other drum is connected to the nylon pennant which is about 200' long. The shockline is then wound up on the drum as needed. This disposes with taking the shockline to the capstan and then making it fast on the bitts.

He has also rigged a short springline on either side of the barge. When he is ready to take the barge "on the hip," he only has to come alongside the barge and throw the eye of his fixed springline over the forward quarter bitts on the tug. When this is fast he can work ahead on his engine and get a headline out and heave up the slack on his surge pennant which is already on the drum of the winch. He has used his experience and thoughtfully worked this out to save a great amount of needless line handling. This is a good example of "horsepower" in the wheelhouse that I mentioned in a previous chapter.

Chapter 8

The Multiple Tow

Tandem or multiple tows in inland towing are commonplace and are seen as often as the single-barge tow. In ocean or coastwise towing this tandem or triple tow is less often seen. Generally speaking, barges in offshore work tend to be larger, thereby limiting the number of barges needed. Yet many tugs normally tow two or more barges when at sea. Some of these tugs have double- and triple-drum towing winches, and in this case the bight of the tow cable to the after barge lies beneath the barge ahead. It was once common to use what is known as a Christmas tree rig with the barges connected to a single-tow cable ganglialike. The main tow cable had short lengths of chain integrated into it. The individual barge was connected to this by a chain pennant. This provided the necessary weight to keep the cable from raising up under the barges when the tug was pulling. The purpose of this rig was to avoid dragging the tow cable in relatively shallow water. A drawback was the weight and clumsiness of the rig when making and breaking tow, and the necessity of an assisting tug.

When a hawser tug makes a tandem or multiple tow, the barges are usually connected to each other by an intermediate hawser. The intermediate hawsers are in turn connected to the barges at both ends by bridles. These bridles should have retrieving lines affixed to facilitate connecting and disconnecting. When the tug and barges are underway at sea, it is like any other tow.

The difficulty of handling multiple tows is mainly the complexity of the maneuver when getting underway, and stringing the barges—and when shortening up and making fast to them on arrival. Most outside barges are unmanned and the tug may be required to carry out these maneuvers unassisted.

For example, a 1500 h.p. tug towing two 1000-ton barges would connect the tow hawser to the first barge in the normal fashion. The second barge would be connected to the first by about 600' of 7" or 8" intermediate nylon hawser. If the last barge were small or light, a floating intermediate hawser of polypropylene or similar synthetic might be used to advantage.

As with getting underway with a single barge, the problem is one of making fast to the barges in a fashion that will permit them to be dropped from alongside to the short tow position astern with a minimum of lost motion and control.

In inland towing this is no problem as the waters are usually calm enough for the seaman to remain on the barges as long as necessary to slack the hawser. In outside work this may not be practical. A little forethought is required if this maneuver is to be carried out successfully.

When getting underway with two barges it is best to make up at the

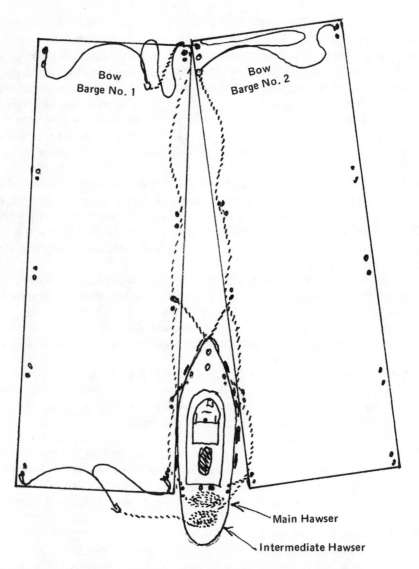

Hawser tug with two barges rigged for dropping astern. Hawsers are secured with rope yarn stoppers outside of the bitts.

dock, with one barge on either side with the bows lashed together forward, and the tug between them. The hawser to the lead barge is stopped off outboard of everything on the barge with light tie lines, and carried down the tug's stern in the usual fashion. The intermediate hawser is also led forward to the bow of the second barge and stopped off by light lines, as is the other hawser. The balance of this is also coiled free for running on the stern of the tug. The bridles connecting to the stern of the lead barge and bow of the second barge should be "pigtailed"; that is, lashed together to avoid the possibility of the shackles falling into the bight of the bridle when the hawser is stretched. The hawser would soon chafe through if this happens.

The tug can then maneuver clear of the dock and drop the tail barge astern of the tug on a short towline until the tug captain is ready to take both the barges in tow. From this position it is easy to stream the rest of the hawser for the after barge. When it comes tight, the tug can let go the first barge and steam ahead until it, too, is astern. When the correct amount of hawser is out, the tug can make fast and proceed with the barges to sea, and stretch the remainder of the hawser when clear of traffic.

There are a number of variations of this maneuver, including lashing the barges together with light lashings that will carry away when swells are encountered. An obvious fault is that no one knows exactly when these "breakaways" will part.

If men can be removed from barges after the intermediate hawser is stretched, or if the barges are manned, this eliminates many of the problems.

In case of a tug fitted with a double-drum towing winch, it is much easier and the tow is made up with the bows of the barges alongside the tug and the sterns lashed together ahead of the tug. The last barge is dropped and when clear of the tug, the brake will be set up on the winch drum so that the barge will turn and line up with the tug. When it is straightened out, the cable can again be slacked until it is far enough astern to permit letting go the lead barge.

When there are more than two barges, the same procedure is followed, provided that the length of the tow is not too great to handle within the confines of the harbor. If this is the case, an assisting tug will be required.

When entering port from seaward, the same procedure is followed as when entering with a single-barge tow. A hawser tug will stop and shorten up, and a tug with a towing winch will heave in the cable to the proper length.

Once inside the harbor, the hawser tug can disconnect the hawser from the bridles on the lead barge, and then "hip up" on the stern of this first barge. Once the tug is fast on the stern of the lead barge, it is

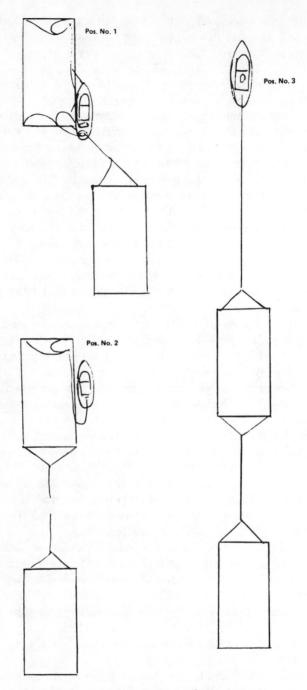

Hawser tug stringing a two-barge tow.

easy to heave the bridles at the stern up on deck with the retrieving line, disconnect the intermediate hawser, and lead it to the tug's capstan to begin heaving easily. It should heave easily on the hawser so the tail barge does not start swinging wildly and so the ends of the barges can be lashed together. Once this is done, the tug can move ahead easily

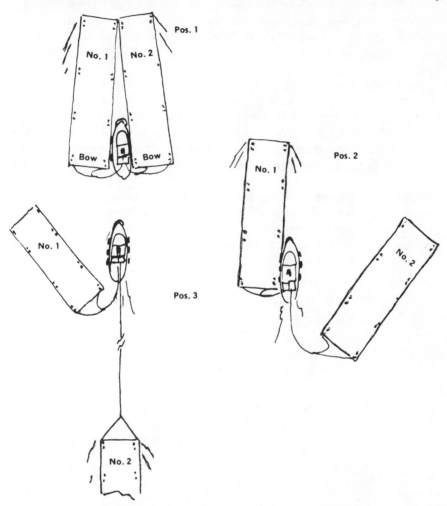

Tug with double-drum towing winch stringing its tow.

and the last barge will fall alongside and can be secured. This is really the whole thing on tandem or multiple tows—get the ends of the barges lashed together and you have the problem solved. If there is a third barge, the procedures are the same except that it may be tied astern of one of the other two barges.

For the tug using a tow cable, the procedure is much the same. Catch one barge, make it fast, and then go after the other one. Often the hawser or tow cable will sink to the bottom and tend to act as a drogue to keep the second and/or third barge more or less anchored while the tug picks them up one at a time.

I often thought (especially when it was blowing and I was chasing a couple of light barges around) that it would be nice to tie one up to a mooring or anchor while I was heaving in the other barge. Unfortunately, moorings are scarce and the ground tackle on most barges is inadequate.

Now there are multiple tows with two or more tugs towing the same object. In most cases it is a drill rig or structure requiring a lot of power. One boat should be designated as the leader and should set the course. The other tug should adjust its hawser length to equal that of the lead boat and then maintain its distance from it, or keep station. This avoids confusion and chances of the tugs haphazardly coming together.

There are, without doubt, many other ways of resolving the problems of handling multiple tows. The application of common sense and a little care in rigging are really all that is required to cope with this problem, or for that matter, any other one you are likely to encounter in the towing business.

Chapter 9

Inland and River Towing

Inland waters of the United States provide many thousands of miles of protected waterways open to navigation. Canals were dredged and maintained for this purpose as far back as Colonial times. This extensive network of rivers and canals carried the waterborne commerce that was

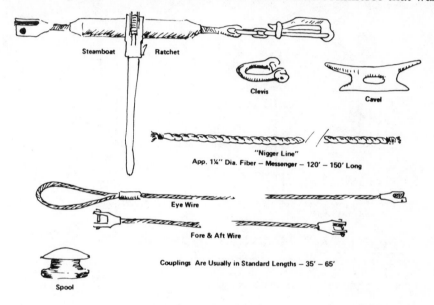

Gear and terminology in use in the Gulf and western rivers.

essential to the development of large areas of the country. Almost 2/3 of the States have waterways that permit some degree of navigation, and the tug and barge are utilized in this endeavor more than any other vessels.

In its own fashion inland navigation is just as demanding as offshore work. The captains, mates and pilots must contend with swift currents, fog, heavy traffic and shifting channels. The lack of wave action permits the tugs to handle much larger tows than they could over open water routes. The handling of these large tows, in a confined area, requires a degree of skill seldom needed in other sectors of the maritime industry.

There are regional distinctions encountered in towboating just as in any other industry. Practices that are in general use in one area may seldom be employed elsewhere. Let's first discuss the pushing of barges, which is the predominant method used in the Gulf/Mississippi area. While it is true that pushing has been in use in other areas, and seems to be increasingly popular, towing the barges astern continues to be the more prevalent method employed elsewhere.

In the Gulf, the vessel that normally pushes its barges ahead is referred to as a "towboat," and the vessel that tows its charges astern is referred to as a "tug." The nomenclature on the inland waters differs too, in other respects. A cleat is known as a "cavel," and shackles are called "clevises" in some areas.

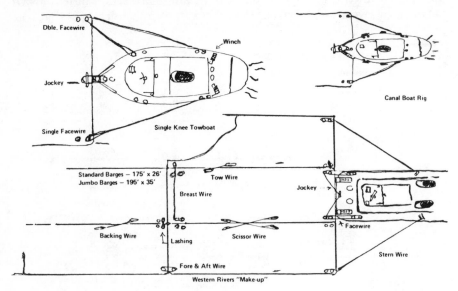

Some typical river and inland water make-ups with towboats pushing.

An old-time riverman said he believed that pushing was a practice that continued on from paddle-wheel steamer days, since most of them on the Mississippi were stern-wheelers and obliged to push the barges ahead of them rather than tow them astern. The flanking rudders were probably borrowed from the paddle-wheelers too, as some of them had additional rudders installed ahead of the paddles for ease in docking downstream.

The towboats engaged in river trade exclusively have evolved as distinct types, and are usually of scow or pram type hull form. They are fitted with push knees and may have two or more propellers set well up under the stern to protect them. The Kort nozzle and flanking rudders are in favor, especially for the larger units. There are conventional hulls that are sometimes fitted with pushing knees, either single or double, and perhaps have the wheelhouse raised in order to provide visibility over a string of light barges.

Double push knees are preferable to a single knee as there is less strain on the facewires. The push knees are to the river towboat the equivalent of the oceangoing tug's tow bitts, and the thrust developed by the towboat's engine is delivered to its barges at this point. The push knees are usually faced with timber or heavy rubber material in order to protect the barge and provide better traction than would be the case if there were direct metal-to-metal contact. Some of the bigger boats are fitted with four knees to distribute the thrust over a wider area. The outer knees on either side are called "stack knees."

There is a lot of shallow-water work. Many of the towboats are trimmed slightly by the bow, so that they will go aground forward instead of getting far enough in on the bank to damage the rudder and propeller.

The cables from the towboat to the barge are called "facewires," and are normally made up on winches, either the hand-action type, or mechanically driven. The winches are usually located midships or further aft. If an additional set of cables is used leading from further aft on the towboat, they are called "sternlines."

When a tug with a single knee is connected up to a barge, a line leading from either side of the bow may be led out to the corner of the barge. These are called jockeys, and prevent the knee from shifting when the steering wheel on the towboat is turned hard over.

The barge made up directly to the towboat is called a "face barge." The farthest barge ahead of the towboat is the "jackstaff barge" and may have a jack staff placed there to steer by. At night a small white light facing aft may be placed there for the same purpose. The outboard barges are called "scabs."

The barges making up a tow are lashed together with cables called "couplings." These couplings are set taut with steamboat ratchets—a type of turnbuckle with a ratchet attached to the barrel. When the steamboat ratchets are tightened they should be rigged so that the lever is pulled inboard. This helps prevent people from falling overboard or between the barges if the ratchet slips.

Debris tends to pack between the barges, and will loosen up the rig of the tow unless lashings are slacked occasionally to clear it away. Often the flow of water to a propeller enclosed by a Kort nozzle will be reduced by an accumulation of similar material. This can be cured by a blast astern on the engines from time to time.

Some of the big towboats that are handling a lot of barges (sometimes as many as 30 or 40 at a time) are using a bow steering unit that is radio-controlled from the wheelhouse. They can safely negotiate bends this way, by themselves, where they might otherwise require assistance.

Under windy conditions a pusher tug might have difficulty con-

trolling a string of light barges. If it has flanking rudders it can tow the
barges backwards. If not, it may be obliged to take the barges in tow
astern or stick them on the bank until the wind abates.

One of the hazards of pushing is parting a facewire. If this should
happen when the tug is pushing at high speed it could result in the
towboat being capsized by the other facewire. This could happen easily,
especially if the engine speed is reduced abruptly. The best thing is to
have another line rigged as a preventer. The barge would then drag the
tug along, bow first, while another facewire is set up.

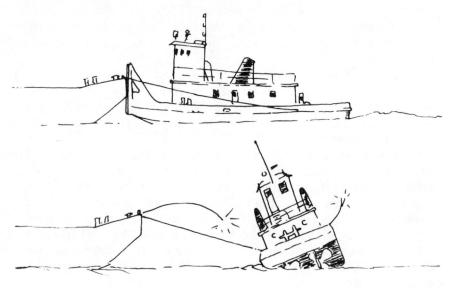

Parting a facewire may lead to a capsize.

Towboats working in some of the canals bordering the coastline
occasionally must cross channels entering from the sea. When the
weather offshore is rough, there is sometimes enough swell running
inside to break up a tow. It is usually better to seek an alternate route,
or take a smaller number of barges across at a time, than to risk losing
the whole tow and have to spend a lot of time getting them together
again. The wake from oceangoing vessels in ship channels can have the
same effect. Even though the burden is on them to avoid this, a towboat with a big tow should keep oncoming traffic advised as to its
location and condition, so the ships will have time to adjust their speed.

Tugs that tow astern in inland waters usually keep their barges on a
short hawser, and may use soft fiber bridles instead of wire. The barges

may be lashed together in a column, or several abreast. When lashed together in a line, the corners of the barges are usually connected by hawsers. Naturally when the tow has to negotiate a sharp bend, the lines at the outboard corner must be slacked.

In some areas vessels transiting canals are restricted as to height.

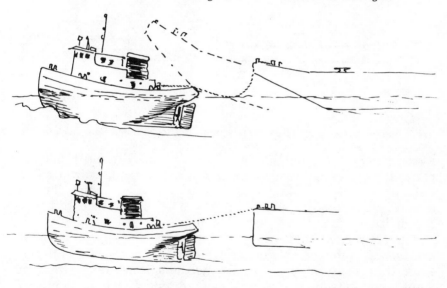

Upper tug in illustration will be damaged by the rake end of the overtaking barge. Tug shown on bottom is towing the barge square-end first to avoid this possibility.

There are dangers to towing "on the string," just as there are those in pushing. A towboat pushing its barges can stop them by backing down. The tug with barges astern cannot do so, and must exercise great care when passing through narrow bridges and areas that are congested with pleasure craft moored or fast at docks along the seawall. The problem is aggravated if there is a fair current pushing the barge along.

There is another danger that has probably been the source of as much damage to tugs as any other. This occurs when a tug towing a lightly loaded rake-end barge astern goes aground. When the tug stops, the rake of the barge will often slide right up on top of the tug, and will sometimes completely demolish it. Often barges built for inland towing have a very short rake to prevent this. Some barges are square-ended on one end, and they are often towed square-end forward for the same

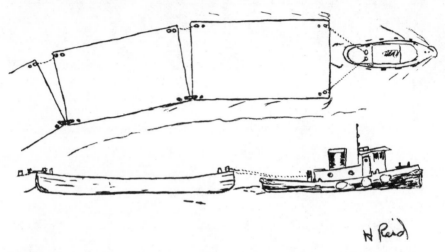

Inland hawser tug making a bend with outboard barge lines slacked.

reason. If the tug should ground, they are likely to hit it, but this is preferable to having the barge crush the tug. It is quite obvious that in order to avoid this hazard the tug's operator must be alert at all times in areas where this might occur. It may even be wiser to take the barge on the hip if the width of the channel permits.

Some tugs make short coastwise trips with the barge on the hawser, and then get into the notch in protected inland waters. Other tugs may work the canals and lakes in the northern states during the warm months and shift to the coastwise routes during the winter months. The increasing variety of work is beginning to require a versatility of the personnel, that sets aside the usual distinction of being either an "inside man" or an "outside man." These are the people in a very interesting employment that enjoy the "best of two worlds."

Chapter 10

The Tug at Sea

Some time ago I was having a discussion with a fellow tugmaster. He offered the opinion that the only skills required of the operator of a tug and its tow, when at sea, were the skills that any adept ship's officer would have. After reflecting a bit, I disagreed. There are special skills that are required in every area of the maritime field. A tactless man would be an unfortunate choice as master of a passenger liner; a poor fisherman, regardless of his other abilities as a mariner, would not cut it as captain of a tuna clipper; and it is not likely that anyone with a limited knowledge of petroleum products and pumping systems would be successful as master of a tanker. Now it is true that a good tugboatman's skills are more apparent while getting underway with a tow, or when shortening up and bringing his barge to the dock. But, while these skills are obvious, there are others that may pass unobserved by one only casually acquainted with towing.

The master of an oceangoing or coastwise tug with a tow has assumed the responsibility of conducting at least two or more vessels to their destination. He will probably be perfectly aware of what is going on aboard the tug, but since the barges are seldom manned on outside routes he must also have a fair idea of how his tow is making out. There are a few other factors, too, that require some understanding based on experience:

1. A tug is much smaller than a conventional freighter and more vulnerable to heavy weather.
2. A tug is usually slower, and so its track is more affected by wind and current.
3. Tugs are corky vessels and celestial navigation requires care and agility on the part of the navigator.
4. A tug's speed will vary more from sea conditions than a freighter's, and so dead reckoning navigation must be done with care.
5. A tug may be taking heavy weather very well, while the barge is being severely damaged.

Tugs are usually wet in even moderate weather. The modest freeboard and tumble-home bulwarks encountered on most of them insure this. They are built this way for good reasons, as they are often obliged to go alongside other vessels when both vessels may be rolling a bit, and the tumble home minimizes the possibility of damage from this type of contact. For stability's sake it is important that the hawser or tow cable be made fast as low as possible, and this in turn accounts for the low freeboard aft. Because of this, the general practice is to stow only a minimal amount of gear on the main deck, and this should be well secured in the lee of the deckhouse.

Any gear that might go adrift should be secured elsewhere. One end of a spare hawser secured on the main deck could easily wash overside through a freeing port and be lost, or even worse, foul the propeller. Spare hawsers and other gear will normally be stowed on the next deck up, or below, to avoid this problem.

Tug and barge in heavy seaway.

In really heavy weather a sharp eye should be kept on sea conditions. Tugs usually have fairly high bulwarks and if washing heavily in a seaway, seas may break aboard the tug faster than the freeing ports allow them to run off. Then the decks may load right to the level of the bulwarks with seawater. This amount of free surface running around on deck can have a drastic effect on stability. This is usually noticeable; the roll of the tug becomes erratic and lazy, and the bow tends to bury into the oncoming swells.

When this situation is encountered, the tug operator should take immediate action to alter it. This is usually best accomplished by either reducing speed or changing course. There are times when circumstances may require both in order to correct the condition. A few tugs have been lost with all hands and this may have been the cause.

Running a tug of moderate size in rough seas without a tow, is probably the most unpleasant part of this business. Tugs are quite bouncy under the best of conditions, and are even more so without the resistance of the tow to steady them. If the weather really makes up, it will usually assure that no one oversleeps, and perhaps all hands will dine on soup and sandwiches until the weather eases.

In older boats the ventilation was usually inadequate, and the watertight doors on the lee side were often kept open to provide a little fresh air. Some of the tugs were fitted with split doors, and the bottom half kept closed with the top left open to catch some breeze. Under the best of circumstances this was a poor practice, but all too often it was the only alternative to suffocation. In boats of this type, whenever a change of course is anticipated which would present the lee side of the moment to the seas, the watch should take a turn below to secure things. The idea of a big sea boiling through an open door might seem funny, but in actual practice it can turn out to be a serious matter. Fortunately, most of the newer boats being built are well equipped in this respect, and many are air-conditioned. This makes the vessels more seaworthy as well as more comfortable.

A tug can plow along and make fine weather of it during a fairly boisterous passage, and at the same time, slam the barge to pieces. This is where judgment and a good pair of binoculars can be of value. If towed too fast in a seaway, the barge can suffer damage, some of it not visible. It is just as likely, though, that a seam will split and the tow will start making water. To avoid this, it is wise to slow down when the barge appears to be laboring.

When a ship or barge is to be towed any distance it is a good idea to paint a highly visible stripe of paint along the waterline forward. If the paint is luminescent, so much the better. A check can then be made day or night for any change in draft.

Heavy following seas can exert severe strains on the towing gear. This is caused by the tendency of the barge to surf a bit as a large sea lifts the stern. The tug will naturally gather way when the strain on the tow hawser or cable eases a bit. The barge will stop surfing as the wave overtakes it, and the tug will be checked with a jerk. Reduction in speed is again the remedy, although an adjustment in the scope of the towing gear may help some, too.

A nylon hawser in good shape will give a fair warning when under strain and approaching the breaking point. An erratic twitching like a cat's tail is the warning sign, and calls for an immediate reduction in engine speed. As a general rule, tow cables should never break clear of the sea except when shortened for entering the harbor. If the bight of the cable seems to be breaking the surface of the water, more scope should be veered or the tug's speed reduced.

The nylon hawser is elastic enough under ordinary conditions to cope with the surge loads. The tow cable, on the other hand, is dependent upon its own catenary for absorbing these shocks. However, when the tug is navigating in relatively shallow water, the tow cable should be shortened enough to insure that it does not drag on the bottom. This is especially likely when there are two or more barges being towed and the cable to the after barges must be slacked sufficiently to pass under the barge ahead. For this reason, it may be necessary to detour around shoal areas that the tug would be able to pass over freely. Dragging a tow cable through rock and sand for even a short time might chew it up enough to make it worthless.

Tugs are corky, and getting good sights is not as easy as it would be on a more stable platform. The motion will frequently cause the compass to oscillate a bit if it is the standard liquid variety. I usually steer courses in 5° increments for this reason. If there is no automatic pilot, it is necessary for each deckhand to steer about double the amount of time he would have to on a freighter, and attention wavers a bit after a

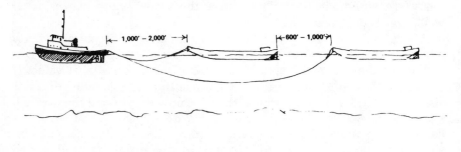

Tug using two cables with a great amount of catenary should avoid shoal areas.

couple of hours. I feel that steering 275° may be a little easier than trying for 273° or 277°. The tug usually will be that much off its track in any event.

A closer eye is required on the actual navigation of the tug than on conventional ships. Since tugs with a tow are going much slower than the average freighter or tanker, the effect of set and drift is proportionately greater. A large light barge, with a fresh wind abeam, can set the tug as much as 10° to leeward of its track. A barge that sheers to one side or the other will have the same effect. Long-range dead reckoning will suffer a lot from this sort of thing, especially since the tug's speed will be more erratic than a ship when sea conditions are changeable.

The electronic navigational systems available now have eased the burden somewhat, but the navigator must still be alert to keep aware of the tug's position at a given moment.

If the tug should have a power failure, or if one is imminent, an effort should be made to turn it away from the track the barge will

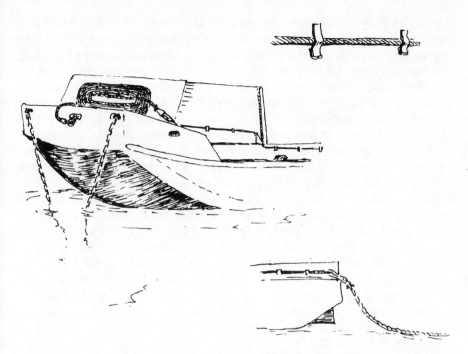

Big ocean barge with a security cable rigged forward. Note light cable connected to floating "pickup" line trailing astern.

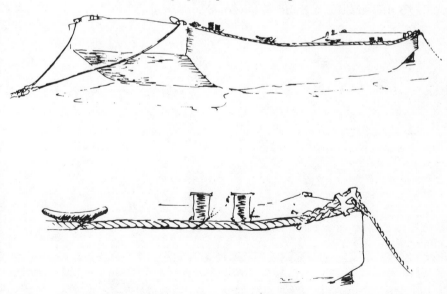

Security hawser rig on smaller oceangoing barge. Hawser is stopped outboard of all deck fittings. Floating "pickup" line trails astern.

take. It is good practice to try to anticipate the effect the wind will have on the barge in this case. If the breakdown occurs in shallow water, the tow cable or hawser may act as a drogue and anchor both tug and barge. If the breakdown takes place in deep water, the weight of the cable may draw the tug and barge together. Having a length of hawser handy to shackle in, in lieu of the cable, will sometimes permit the two units to drift clear of each other and avoid having to cast the barge adrift to protect the tug and barge from heavy damage.

On barges being towed over long routes, it is fairly common to rig an insurance hawser. This is a length of hawser shackled into its own bridle or pennant on the bow of the barge, and led down either side of the barge. It should be lashed in place with light stoppers outboard of everything. The outboard end should have a thimble. A length of floating line should be made fast to the outboard end; this is allowed to trail astern of the barge. It should be strong enough to take the strain of breaking the safety hawser out of its stoppers and heave it on board the tug. Usually 5" or 6" polypropylene is a good size, and should trail behind about 100 feet. This will permit the tug to pick up the barge's emergency hawser and connect up without going alongside the barge if it does go adrift. Errors are often made before a voyage is begun, and negligence is frequently repaid with a vengeance. The reward of a diligent skipper is the confidence he feels when the weather makes up and he feels secure in the knowledge that every reasonable effort has been made to prepare the tug and barge for their voyage.

Chapter 11

Salvage and Rescue

The word salvage conjures up visions of "romance and adventure." While it frequently has elements of adventure, it usually lacks the "romance." Imagine, if you can, how romantic it would be to wallow around in a sea of crude oil while trying to assist a grounded tanker with a ruptured cargo tank. While not often this messy, it can be a risky and delicate task; and requires judgment and experience under the best of circumstance.

Men have been engaged in efforts to salvage ships and their cargoes ever since ships began trading and/or raiding. Apparently the Dutch were the first to employ the steam tug in this activity. The Wijsberg Co. was established in Holland in 1826 to engage in this work, and I understand the parent company is still active in the field at present.

The term salvage is rather inclusive and applies equally to the act of picking up a skiff that has broken its moorings, or refloating a stranded supertanker. For our purposes, however, it would be best to consider it as applying only to vessels of 100 gross tons or more.

The type of salvage that a tug might be called upon to engage in normally breaks down into two categories. "Salvage" per se is understood to refer to a situation where the tug assists in refloating a vessel stranded or aground. The term "rescue" is used to indicate the towage of a vessel adrift to a safe port. In order to avoid confusion, we will deal with each subject in turn.

Vessels can go aground for various reasons. Usually it is the result of an error in navigation. Our concern here is not the cause, but the remedy; in salvage terms this is referred to as "refloating" a vessel. Usually tugs are the first commercial vessels called upon to assist a ship after it has gone ashore. If the vessel is not too hard aground and has not suffered severe bottom damage, tugs are often able to refloat the vessel by pulling it into deeper water.

If the vessel is hard aground, refloating her may require lightening the ship by removal of cargo and bunkers, and use of beach gear. If there is extensive bottom damage it may be necessary to use pumps, compressors, and divers to patch the ship enough to keep it afloat once it is in deeper water.

When this is the case, it is likely that the services of a regular salvage vessel will be called upon, providing that the value of the vessel and its cargo are sufficient to justify the cost involved.

71

A salvor's services are costly. There are several reasons for this. In the first place, salvage vessels are usually larger than the ordinary tug, frequently being ex-navy fleet tugs fitted out with all the necessary gear, and carrying a large crew skilled in the use of this equipment. Another factor to be considered is that salvage contracts are usually "no-cure/no-pay" agreements. Since an undertaking of this sort is often rather speculative, the salvor must try to cover other losses and allow for unanticipated costs.

Tug floating a nylon hawser to small freight aground in shallow area. Truck inner tubes keep hawser from fouling on bottom.

When a tug is sent to assist a ship aground, it is more than likely located where it is supposed to be, but do not be surprised if it is not. Sometimes little discrepancies like this caused the ship to go aground in the first place.

It is helpful if someone on the tug is familiar with the general area and can anticipate the conditions to be expected. A knowledge of the average wind, sea and current set, as well as the nature of the bottom can prove to be very valuable on occasion.

If the grounded vessel is deep-draft, there is usually enough water for the tug to work in close and pass a hawser aboard without any trouble. If, however, the ship is small or light, she may have been driven so far ashore that it is impossible for the tug to get near. This is when a shoulder type Lyle gun, or a good small boat, comes in handy.

On one occasion, a seaman from a Japanese tuna boat swam out with a light line to my tug, after which we successfully connected up and refloated the vessel. This sort of thing is definitely not recommended, especially if other alternatives are possible. A heavy-duty, inflatable boat (like a Zodiac) with a good outboard motor would be much less hazardous.

When the vessel is aground in shallow water, one of the problems is to get the hawser aboard. Unless the hawser is of the floating type, or the bottom is smooth, you can depend on it to foul on rocks, coral or debris. Even a very stout messenger will part under these circumstances. You can remedy this by carrying enough heavy-duty truck inner tubes and a hose and adapter to inflate them from the tug's compressor. The tubes, lashed to the hawser at intervals as it is paid out, will keep the hawser off the bottom until it can be passed aboard.

Different conditions sometimes require different solutions. Ships driven aground on nearly level sandy or mud bottoms may require lightening to refloat. In spite of this, however, they will keep working themselves further ashore unless anchors are led out, or the ship is ballasted to prevent it. At times a tug lashed alongside, where its wheel-wash tends to blow away the sand or mud, is more effective than pulling at long range on a hawser.

A vessel aground on coral bottom will frequently grind the coral down to powder (especially if there is a little sea running) and will come free even when the situation looks very unpromising. The object is to get a small amount of motion going and sustain it. This will very often pay off.

I have seen vessels quite high up on rounded, smooth rocks come off with surprising ease, especially if the bottom is steep-to.

Watch the tides and make maximum effort during the peak of the flood. Remember that a bit of sea can be used to advantage if the vessel begins to move at all. Just keep the vessel moving. If there is a salvage master aboard he will know how to use the tug to best advantage. Otherwise, the tug captain should try pulling from every possible angle until he discovers one that causes the ship to start wiggling.

A word of caution: Salvage can be risky work. Extreme vigilance at all times is important. A ship can come unstuck with astonishing speed and an error at this time can undo every one's efforts, as well as cause additional injury to equipment or personnel.

If there is more than one tug pulling on the ship, and they are working close together, the hawser lengths should be equal. Tugs are ordinarily well fendered, and an occasional bump if they come together is not likely to do serious damage. But the tug coming in contact with tight nylon hawser is something else, and the results of this type of contact are best left to the imagination.

When a tug is pulling on a vessel aground, it is working in a situation where the machinery is under heavy load and the propeller slip is 100%; there may have to be some adjustment in engine speed to avoid overheating the engine.

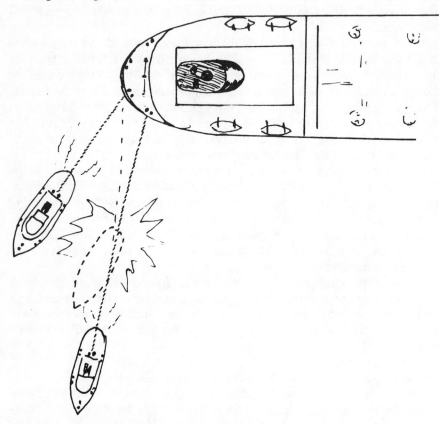

Danger! Both tugs should have hawsers of similar length to avoid this type of contact.

Should tugs working close together come in contact, it is sometimes better to put the tug's wheel hard over in the opposite direction from where the operator wishes to go. The resulting wheelwash will usually skid the tug over somewhat before it starts to turn. The tug can then straighten up as needed.

If a tug is required to make a rescue tow of a ship adrift, the master will probably receive a description of the vessel, covering its name, tonnage and last known position. It is wise for him to try to find out as much as possible about the vessel at that point. He should, for example, try to learn the nature of the damage, draft, length overall, and the type of radio equipment on board.

With this pertinent information in hand he should check the tug to make sure everything needed is on board. Hopefully the tug will have up-to-date charts of the area, as well as pilot charts and sailing directions. All the radio and navigational gear should be in good order, as well as the radar. It is wise to determine if other stores are adequate: fuel, water, food, searchlight bulbs, first-aid supplies, etc.

After satisfying himself that the stores are adequate and navigational equipment complete, the captain should turn his attention to deck gear required to take the ship in tow. There should be a number of spare shackles on board, a spare tow hawser, bridles adequate for the job and, if possible, a spare set. There should also be at least one good messenger line (1¼" to 1½" in diameter and 40 to 50 fathoms long) and several extra-long heaving lines. It is important for the tug to have a couple of good Walkie-Talkies (CB or VHF) with spare batteries.

Some towing companies keep a shoulder-held line-throwing gun on standby for this sort of job. But, generally speaking, if it is too rough to get close enough to pass a heaving line aboard, it is too rough to attempt hooking up and should not be attempted unless the vessel is in danger of going ashore.

When the tug is ready to get underway, the next problem confronting the captain is to find the vessel. If the tug can establish radio contact with the ship, this eliminates the problem of keeping track of its position. When this is impossible, the tug is obliged to depend on relayed information, and frequently this is scanty. All too often the only contact the tug will have with a ship will be through the agents or charterers, and secondhand at that. If this is the case, the tug's captain had better prepare to do some ship hunting.

When there has been any continuity in the ship's position reports, it is easier to predict the position of contact with fair accuracy. Should the positions given be sparse or weird, the best thing is to take the vessel's last firm position and try to figure the vessel's drift by using the pilot charts. This is when it is useful to know something about the vessel's loaded condition. A lightly laden ship will naturally drift faster in fresh winds than one that is deep-loaded. It should be remembered that vessels do not just drift downwind, but tend to work ahead or astern as they drift.

If a search is going to be required, the tug should plot a ladder type pattern, starting a bit to weather of the vessel's probable position, and work down the probable line of drift that the vessel will take. I figure on ten miles as being about the maximum range at which one can be

able to pick another vessel with surety from a tug, and lay out the legs
about 20 miles apart, and at right angles to the driftline. The length of
the legs may be increased as the track extends, to permit the tug to
cover the area in which the vessel is liable to be found. This is tedious,
but usually works. Much time could be saved if a drifting ship would
simply turn on its searchlight and aim it straight up. This can be seen
for miles at night.

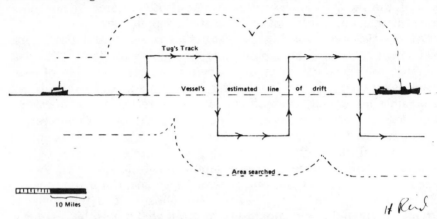

A ladder search pattern.

A searchlight directed upward can be seen for miles at sea and can help
locate a vessel adrift

After the ship is located, a decision must be made on what type of hookup is to be used. If the ship has power on deck and the tow is to be long, it would probably be best to stop off an anchor and connect the tug's tow hawser or cable into the ship's anchor chain. When the chain is slacked out from one to three shots, it will take up a lot of the shock from the surging and deal with the problem of chafe at the same time. Should the situation not permit this, the preparation to pass the bridles on board should be made.

Tug has finished connecting to dead ship and getting ready to stream the hawser.

Rescue tug entering harbor with an assisting tug astern of dead ship.

Before attempting anything, all gear should be laid out in readiness and an estimate made of the vessel's drift relative to the tug's. Unless the sea is rather calm, it is best to avoid contact between the two vessels. I usually try to position the tug ahead of the vessel, stern to bow, and either a bit to leeward or weather, depending on which is drifting faster. This is done in order to minimize the amount of maneuvering required while connecting up. It should be remembered that a tug is not as responsive to rudder or engine when maneuvering in a seaway as it would be in the harbor, and a little more room must be allowed to compensate for this.

If no communication has been established with the ship, a Walkie-Talkie should be sent up with the first heaving line. The end of the messenger line should be bent onto the heaving line and the bridles (if used) and the hawser heaved on board and secured. When bridles are used, the chocks should be greased to guard against chafe.

Once the ship is in tow and brought to course, some adjustment in speed may be required. Large, deep-laden ships are more likely to give trouble than others, as they have a tendency to sheer. Sometimes this can be corrected by moderating the speed of the tug.

When a tug has a dead ship in tow and is arriving at its destination, the tow will be shortened in the normal fashion. Unless the entrance channel is a straight shot, and of ample width, it is wise to call ahead and request an assisting tug.

Salvage operations and rescue tows are not everyday occurrences. But they do happen often enough so that practically every tug will be called upon on some occasion to assist a vessel in distress. As mentioned before, "romance" is usually in short supply, but this is often compensated by the satisfaction one feels after a job well done.

Chapter 12

Anchor Work

The versatility of tugs has often been put to the test. This is especially true in the offshore oil industry where tugs participate in practically every phase of drilling and production. The rapid development of the tug itself over the last few years owes much to the dynamic, and even aggressive, approach of the operators who provide services in this sector of the marine field.

Some of the new tugs coming out are hybrids that somewhat resemble supply boats, but have been "beefed" up to withstand the heavier demands of towing and, of course, have machinery aboard developing more power.

A large part of the equipment and supplies is barged to the locations and the drill rigs themselves are usually spotted with tugs.

Anchor running is an operation more or less typical of the work peculiar to the offshore industry, and for this reason I have chosen to discuss this operation. Many of the tugs working in areas where there are offshore oil operations are fitted with additional gear necessary for this employment. Once a well is producing, a pipeline must be laid underwater which will carry the product to a storage facility. As one would imagine, this requires miles and miles of pipeline in an active field.

This pipeline is laid from barges where the entire process of welding it together, coating it, and sliding it into the sea, takes place. The barges are constantly moving as this work goes on. The position of the barge is controlled by anchors that are spotted ahead and astern of it. These anchors are attached to cables wound on the drum of special anchor winches that are driven through torque converters that can pay out and heave in the anchor wires at predetermined settings.

Tugs are used to shift these anchors as the barge moves slowly ahead. The anchors are rigged with a trip-wire pennant that passes through a hole in the buoy and has an eye at the outboard end. When it is necessary to shift the anchor, the tug will connect a cable from its own winch into the anchor pennant, and heave away until the anchor is close aboard. It will then steam off in the required direction. The pennant, of course, slides through the hole in the middle of the buoy.

Some tugs heave the anchor from an aperture cut in the forward bulwarks fitted with rollers. The tug's cable is led through a series of fairleads so it can be connected to the anchor pennant.

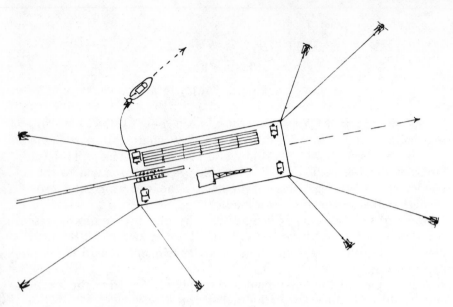

A pipeline barge at work with anchors laid. Tug is shifting one anchor.

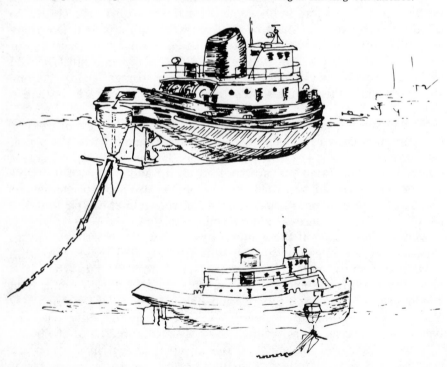

(Top) Tug with stern chock with anchor heaved up, ready to move out. (Bottom) Older type tug with anchor heaved through a bow chock.

Newer tugs are generally fitted out to work over the stern, and are often fitted with a double-drum towing winch. One drum has a regular tow cable wound on it for barge work. The other will usually have the level wind removed and have a short length of lighter cable wound on it to hook into the anchor pennant. Naturally these tugs have an after-control station and most of them are twin-screw as they must stay in position when it is blowing and have to back down on the buoy to pick up the anchor pennant.

Tugs doing this work should be fitted with a gyrocompass in order to be able to proceed in the direction ordered without having to calculate compass error. A P.A. System and good lighting on deck are essential as a close coordination of effort is required, and good visibility is necessary to avoid accidents when working at night.

The tug's movement is controlled by the barge master who works from a chart of the area. He plots the location where the anchors are to be dropped. He also monitors the tug's position on radar, and directs it by VHF radio. For example, the tug will receive orders to pick up a certain anchor. This will be done, and the tug will then be ordered to proceed in a given direction while the anchor cable is payed out or heaved in. When the tug is over the new position where the anchor is to be placed, it will be notified and can then slack out the anchor pennant and disconnect its cable.

The pipeline barge will normally continue working right around the clock as long as weather permits. This means, of course, that the tug is liable to see some pretty rough going, especially in areas where heavy weather is often encountered. A tug assigned to this task will be kept quite busy because from six to eight anchors are used to keep the barges in position as they move along.

It may seem, at first, that a captain in charge of a tug engaged in this type of operation is not required to have the degree of skill required elsewhere in the towing industry. But, upon reflection, it occurs that the tug is being used as part of a team effort and requires plenty of ability and a bit of "guts" on the part of the tug crew if the ultimate purpose of the operation is to be achieved.

As a matter of fact, it is generally conceded that some of the best "boathandlers" in the entire towing industry have done their "post-graduate" work in the offshore oil fields. As proof of this, one may see American tug crews working all over the world, even where crews of other nationalities could be employed at far less cost.

Chapter 13

Handling the Big, Big Barge

In recent years the economy of the towing operation has encouraged the construction of increasingly larger barges. These have proven successful in moving bulk cargoes over fairly lengthy routes, and this trend is likely to continue.

For the sake of definition, let us assume that a barge of a burden exceeding 20,000 deadweight tons is a "big, big barge." Most seagoing barges of this size will likely have either a model bow or a spoon bow.

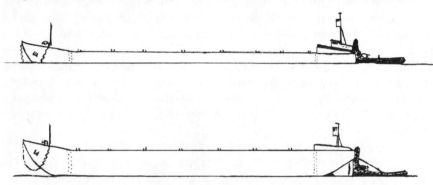

Typical tug and big barge showing barge in loaded and light position.

There will be a notch in the stern to permit the tug to push it. It is also apt to have fairly adequate ground tackle, and adjustable skegs to prevent yawing. There should be ladders inset on the fore and aft sides and in the towing notch to permit the crew to board safely. There may be "Panama" or "pocket" chocks installed about the freeboard to aid assisting tugs to make fast alongside. There should be a permanently rigged security hawser, and whatever is required for the tug to make up in the notch.

The tugs that handle these big, big barges may tow them astern or push them, according to circumstances. Often when the barge is loaded and the sea is not too rough, they will push them. When weather makes up, the tug will take the barge on a towline. A light barge may be pushed if the notch is deep enough for the tug to get in without incurring damage from the after rake, and if the wheelhouse is high enough for the tug's operator to see over the barge. In some cases the pilothouse can be raised, and in others there is a special bridge for navigating when pushing a light barge. When this is not the case, it may be necessary for the tug to handle a light or partially loaded big, big barge on the string.

When in the notch and pushing, the tug will naturally have more control than when towing the barge astern. It will be able to steer ahead, back, and turn the barge. But with a large, deep-loaded barge, with too much way on it, the "twin-screw effect" (assuming the tug is twin-screw) is largely diminished. The screws in relation to the size of

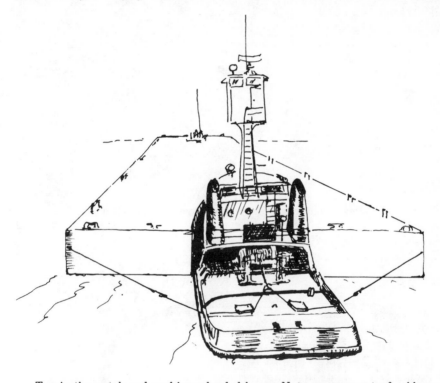

Tug in the notch and pushing a loaded barge. Note arrangement of cables.

the barge are set quite close together and simply lack the leverage to "twist" it as they would a smaller barge.

When blowing, the effect of the wind on the exposed freeboard of a light barge may be so great that the tug will not be able to control the barge from the pushing position and may have to abandon the notch in order to take the barge in tow astern.

When light or partially loaded, these barges normally tow beautifully. But when loaded, almost all of them have a strong tendency to sheer. This is really the crux of the problem. At sea with adequate room, this is more of an inconvenience than a hazard. In close quarters this is

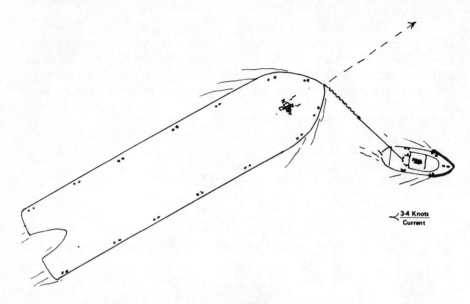

Tripping situation with a big, big barge on a short towline.

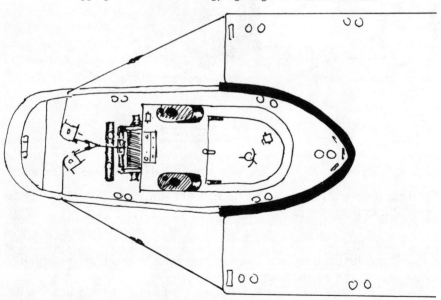

Tug in notch. Deck arrangement of tug pushing big, big barge. Note tug's tow cable connected to "facewires."

another matter, and is the principal cause of most accidents that occur when handling these monster-sized barges.

There are additional factors that contribute in one degree or other to the risk involved in handling larger carriers. First of all, there is the sheer mass of the barge whose displacement may be 25—30 times that of the tug. A 6000 h.p. tug may only displace twice as much as a 1500 h.p. tug. The smaller tug may handle barges whose displacement (perhaps at maximum) is only 10—15 times that of the tug's. There is ample power in the 6000 h.p. unit, but the tug may simply lack the weight to be able to apply it effectively.

In addition to the mass involved when loaded, these big barges expose a tremendous area of water plane. This can often work to the disadvantage of the tug trying to turn them sharply on a short towline. All too often the vessels simply tend to accelerate along the initial line of advance, and may overpower the tug. If the tug tries to counter this by coming full ahead with the wheel hard over, it may be capsized.

The force developed by a mass in motion tends to expand proportionately as size increases. As the speed doubles, the effect is more or less squared. Imagine if you can, the comparative effect in the forces generated when the speed of a 10,000-ton barge doubles with that of a 20,000-ton barge. These are the forces that a tug handling these barges must overcome in order to exercise effective control over its charge.

The most dangerous situation occurs when a tug is entering or leaving the harbor with a big, big barge deep-loaded on a short towline. If the tug is unassisted, it must guard against the barge's tendency to accelerate as the tug changes course. It must avoid, at any cost, getting too much speed on the barge which would generate the kind of forces that it would be impossible for the tug to overcome. It is probable that in narrow waterways a speed greater than 3½—4 knots through the water would be excessive with a really big, deep-loaded barge on a towline.

There are a number of places (e.g., the passes entering the Mississippi) where a tug may have to overcome a current of 3—5 knots. A little too much power applied can result in a loss of control, particularly if the barge's bow starts "sailing" crosscurrent.

There are no simple answers to these problems which confront a tugmaster towing the extremely heavy barges. Often, the owners themselves are ignorant of the amount of skill and judgment required to consistently deliver the vessels safely to their destination. The tugmaster can only use his experience to clearly define his "limits of control" and insist that his judgment be respected in that regard.

Until such a time as gear is developed that will aid the tug in controlling its charge from taking these scary sheers when handling on a short towline, the operator is obliged to consider a few precautions:

1. Have an assisting tug, if possible.
2. Avoid letting the barge gather too much way.
3. Avoid using too short a tow hawser.
4. When entering a river or inlet it may prove wiser to wait for a favorable tide which might abate the current.
5. Station a man to stand by the barge's anchor.

This situation could be avoided if the barge could enter the channel with the tug in the notch, but often sea conditions prohibit this. When this problem is resolved, the size of barges will probably continue to increase, and it may be that the time is not far off when seagoing barges capable of carrying 100,000 tons deadweight will be seen.

Until such a time as these problems are resolved, either by adequate bow and stern thrusters, braking flaps, or stern anchors, it is likely that the tugmaster will have to continue depending on his own judgment to keep his charges safe from harm.

Chapter 14

Tips on Towing

One accumulates much miscellaneous information over the years. It may not fall into any particular category, but hopefully will be of real value to someone, sometime. I will try to put down some of this related and unrelated data as it occurs to me, rather than in order of importance.

The young man interested in a career in the marine field will find much more opportunity on tugs than he will on the conventional ships, at least at the time of this writing. Conditions are improving, wages are getting better all the time, and the towing business is currently the most viable sector of the entire U.S. Merchant Marine.

Before investing too much time, a young fellow starting out as a deckhand or ordinary seaman should check to determine that his physical and visual capabilities will permit him to progress professionally. If he has a visual deficiency, or other failing that would prohibit his advancement in the deck department, he might choose to get into the engineering end where the requirements are not as strict.

If one enjoys working on the tugs and intends to continue working in the industry, he should take the steps that lead to advancement. As soon as he has the necessary time to qualify for a better berth, the required effort should be made to prepare for the examination. It is rewarding financially and satisfying personally.

The young man who already has a license and is interested in finding employment within the towing industry can pick and choose to a certain extent. And he should. New manning and licensing requirements for the industry are already in effect. Companies operating big tugs that are towing big barges are constantly looking for fresh talent. This may not be the best place for a young man with a Third Mates License to start. No one is likely to let a new young mate do any maneuvering with a 4000—6000 h.p. tug, and once the routine is established an operation of this sort seldom varies. Perhaps he would be better off initially looking for a job with a smaller company, operating smaller tugs involved in more diverse activities. He will usually learn more and faster, and in addition, will be obliged to handle the tugs. This is really the name of the game: "Boathandling."

I have spent time on freighters, tankers, fishing vessels and tugs. Each type of operation has its own particular area of expertise. I feel that the standard of seamanship encountered on a well-run tug is usually the equal, or superior to, any that one may expect to find in the maritime industry. I have also noticed that an overbearing and officious officer seldom reaps the benefit of this professional excellence.

A young man who finds himself appointed as captain of a tug is probably a pretty fair handler, and will be knowledgeable about the mechanics of the business. Now he should acquaint himself with some of his additional responsibilities. This comes under the heading of "ship's business." There is plenty of information on this subject, and anyone sailing as master should acquire the material that will provide him with the information needed.

A well-kept log on any vessel performs an important function, especially in cases involving accident or injury. It is often entered as evidence at court that may clear the tug, its crew, and its owners from accusations of wrongdoing. The log should be punctilious on matters relating to navigation of the tug, but avoid observations of a personal nature and trivia. Only information that is germane to the operation of the vessel, its crew, or its tow should be recorded. A log is not a personal journal.

The nature of the towing business frequently requires tugs to tow barges, ships, dredges, and other craft on short notice. On many occasions the captain of the tug may never have seen this equipment before. The tug's master should take the time to inspect it carefully. Naturally a complete survey is not possible, but he should look it over thoroughly enough to be able to make a log entry as follows:

"Examined Barges _____ at _____ hr. and found same in apparently seaworthy condition."

If he cannot honestly make a log entry to this effect, he should notify the tug's owners and advise them so. If the owners insist that the barge be towed in spite of the negative opinion of its seaworthiness, the tugmaster should then seek a waiver of responsibility from the owner or operator of the equipment to be towed. A log entry relating to the details should be made. Should a loss occur, this entry will serve to point the finger at the real culprit.

In towing operations a certain amount of damage is unavoidable. This is a high risk business. Some damage results from human error; other damages are the inevitable consequence of circumstances beyond anyone's control. Professional towing companies know this and expect a certain amount of it to occur. "Johnny-Come-Latelys" from other sectors of the maritime field are often ignorant of this. A minor dent that would be overlooked by a bona fide operator will require a 20-page report to amateurs. Avoid seeking employment with them for this reason. It is better to wait until such companies have been in the business for a few years.

When damage does occur, be frank and make the appropriate log entry. Advise the tug's owners or operators promptly so that they can take steps to protect themselves. For example, you may put a dent in an over-age tanker operated by a company with home offices located in "Outer Mongolia." If the damage is not promptly surveyed, your company will more than likely receive a bill for repairs to damages that have accumulated during the past five years.

There are quite a few "tricks to the trade," as listed below:

1. If a single-screw tug is required to put a man on board an anchored ship, and it is rough, it is a good idea to put up a line from the bow of the tug, but leading aft like a spring. This will enable the tug to stay in position until he is safely aboard the vessel.

2. In hazy or foggy weather, a tug with a long tow strung out behind it might shorten up a bit if weather conditions permit. Fishing vessels and small craft may not notice the barge, and attempt to cross between the tug and its tow.

3. In foreign ports, particularly where unemployment runs high, check all the barge's compartments for stowaways. This is where you will find them—not on the tug; but "you" are still responsible for them when you arrive at the next port.

4. A tug is required to carry a first-aid kit for the crew. The tug's captain should see that one is on board for the tug as well: a few sacks of cement, a tarpaulin, some plywood, and a few lengths of threaded rod with nuts and washers.

There is an excellent hydraulic cement for sealing small holes that sets under water in about three minutes. It is called "Waterplug." Some of this product should be kept on hand for emergencies.

5. As mentioned before, a 2" or 3" gasoline or diesel-driven centrifugal pump, complete with hose strainer and foot valve may be worth its weight in gold. Many tugs (barges, too) have been saved by having one on board.

6. Bosuns' lockers on tugs are often poorly ventilated. To avoid the danger of fire or spontaneous combustion, it might be better to stow the paints and thinners on the boat deck in a suitable locker of their own.

7. Periodically the tug's mate or captain should make a round, checking the above-deck structure for watertightness. The list of items to be checked would include gaskets on watertight doors and portlights, the dogs on the doors and ports, all hatches and openings that have covers. Also, take a look at the ball checks in the vents of various tanks.

8. When ships, dredges, and other unmanned vessels with engine rooms are being towed, the tug's chief engineer should take a turn below to make sure that all is secure. A valve might have been left open that could result in the loss of the vessel.

9. When preparing to tow a ship for any distance, it is often a good idea to have a piece of heavy-duty pipe or plate welded on the stem where the bridles will rub. This will protect both the ship's bow and the bridles from wear.

10. The deck department should have its own tools. Small hand tools last longer when kept in the captain or mate's room. Larger tools, such as crowbars, mauls and large wrenches, should be kept in a safe place accessible when making and breaking tow.

11. A short wire bridle about 6'—8' long, with a large eye at one end and a thimble eye at the other, is handy for getting a line on a drifting barge at sea. One man can handle it on the barge, and it will serve its purpose until better arrangements can be made.

12. An old anchor chain and length of worn hawser might keep a tug off the beach if the engine breaks down. Even if the anchor is lost in the process, it is still a bargain. I like to keep at least one expendable anchor on hand.

13. Small boat-flasher depth-sounders, with self-contained batteries, are inexpensive. The transducer can be made fast to a pole and lashed over the side. They may be useful when working on a salvage in dirty water where there is much shoaling.

14. Local knowledge is the tugboatman's stock in trade, and he should observe current sets, tidal effects, wind and weather, and compare notes with others operating in the same area.

15. A diver's face mask and set of swim fins may help clear a line from the wheel. A set of scuba gear is handy if there is someone on board experienced in using it. Saw wires with finger loops cut a tightly wound hawser quite well. A hacksaw works better than a knife for this, also.

16. When new and inexperienced deckhands come on board, some time should be spent in instruction on making lines fast properly, throwing a heaving line, and making and breaking tow. Some captains stick a paintbrush or a chipping hammer in their hands when they step aboard, neglecting to acquaint them with some of their other duties in preparation for the time to get underway with a barge.

17. At times, even an experienced crewman does not know how to make a towboatman's hitch, or make a tow hawser fast on the bitts properly. They should be instructed on how to do it if this is the case.

18. Tugs are usually uninspected vessels, and are not required to stage fire and boat drills. But everyone should know the location of the fire extinguishers and fire stations. The fire pumps, life raft and buoyant apparatus should be tested periodically. Spending a few minutes this way each week could save lives later on.

19. Battery-powered running lights seldom work up to specifica-

tions, even the Coast Guard approved type. Change batteries frequently and log it; it might save a fine.

20. Some tugs heavily fendered with tires may flip them on board to save the paint on the topsides when making a run outside. Sometimes it is as rough one mile offshore as it is 20 miles at sea. The fenders may obstruct the flow of water to the freeing ports, causing the decks to load up with water. If this happens, it is better to slip the tires over again, or remove them to avoid having too much free surface running around on deck.

21. When towing in coastwise or inland waters at night, especially during weekends and holidays, extra care must be taken of the yachts and small boat traffic one may encounter. Many weekend sailors are not aware of what a tug's towing lights mean, and may unwittingly cause an accident. Do not hesitate to use the spotlight to illuminate the barge, or blow the whistle with plenty of time to spare so that these smaller boats can get clear.

22. On several occasions I have towed ships using other ships. I set out to do this deliberately. In each instance a nylon tow hawser was used; this was connected to chain bridles on the vessel being towed, and shackled into a short length of chain that passed through the stern chock of the vessel doing the towing. The voyages were all concluded successfully, in spite of encountering some fairly heavy weather during 2000—3000-mile tows. I feel that unless an automatic towing winch were installed, the nylon tow hawser would be preferable to attempting a similar tow with a cable. Passing a nylon hawser from one ship to another is easily accomplished with the motor lifeboat, and the ships can avoid coming into close quarters while connecting up.

In recent years the towing industry has attracted a lot of men from big ships who hold ocean licenses. Some of them suffer from an inferiority complex when they compare the size of their tug with the large size of the vessels they served on before. I doubt that this is justified.

A friend and former employer, who operates tugs as well as conventional ships, once said, "Shipping and towing are different businesses. But, from a practical point of view, I would rather give command of one of my ships to one of my tugmasters than attempt to put one of my shipmasters in charge of a tug."

Index

Anchor, 14
  rode, 14, 27
  work, 79-81
    pipeline barge, schematic, 80

Barge, 11-15
  bitts, 13
  description of, 11
  ground tackle, 14-15
  gusset knees, 12-13
  handling, 41-47
    docking, 44
    "hip up," 50, 55
    large type, 81-86
    "on the hip," 41, 42, 52
    "on the string," 45
    "springing," 43
  inland, 11, 59-64
  jackstaff, 61
  multiple tow, 53-58
  offshore, 11
  scow hull, 12
  skeg, 12, 14
Bethlehem Steel Company, 20
Bitts, 8, 13, 15, 25, 31, 41, 42, 43, 45, 52, 54
Bollard pull, 8, 19
Bridle, 16, 46, 48, 53, 57, 78
  chain, 21
  "pigtailed," 55
  schematic, 22
  wire cable, 21
Bulwark, 8, 12, 65
Bureau of Marine Inspection, 12

Cable, tow, 58
  chart of strengths, 20
  fittings, 21, 22, 23, 24

Capstan, 42, 49, 52, 57
Cavel, 59
Charlotte Dundas, 1
  (*See also* Tug, steam)
Chock, "bull-nose," 39
Clevis, 59

Eye wire, 59

Facewire, 60, 84
  parting of, 62
Fender systems, 16, 27, 29, 32
  bow, schematic, 28
Fittings, terminal, 21
  schematic, 22, 23

Gear, towing, 16-29
  barge, 14-15
  bridles, 16, 21
  chafing gear, 16
  chain stoppers, 26
  fender systems, 16, 27, 29
    schematic, 28
  fittings, 21
  gob line, 29
  hawser, 3, 19, 25
    size chart, 9
    strength chart, 18
  heaving lines, 16, 18
  inland (*See* Inland service)
  ladders, 27
  Norman pin, 26, 29
  shackles, 16, 24
    schematic, 23
  straps, 26, 27
  supplementary, 16
  surge pennant, 16
  tow cable (*continued*)

Gear, tow cable (*continued*)
   fittings, 21
   strengths chart, 20
   working lines, 16, 18, 19, 26, 27
   (*See also* individual listings)
Gusset knee, 12
   schematic, 13
Gyrocompass, 81

Harbor tugs, 30
   control station, 34
Hawser, 16, 19, 25
   insurance, 70, 82
   intermediate, 54, 55, 57
   length, 17, 19
     schematic, 74
   main, 54
   shackles, schematic, 23
   size, chart, 9
   strength, fiber rope, table, 18
   synthetic fiber, 3
Headline, 38, 39, 41, 42, 48
Heaving lines, 16

Inland service, 6, 59-64
   barge, pushing, 59-63
   canal boat rig, schematic, 60
   couplings, 61
   face barge, 61
   gear, 59
   jackstaff barge, 61
   jockeys, 60-61
   "on the string," 63
   push knee, 60-61
   single knee towboat, schematic, 60
   towboat, 60
   tug, 60

Jackstaff barge, 61
Jockeys, 60, 61

Kort nozzle, 8
   description, 3
   rudder on tug, 4
   towboat, river, 4, 60, 61

Ladders, aluminum, 27
Log entry, 88-89
Lyle gun, 73

Merchant Marine, 2, 4, 87
Messenger, 16, 26, 49, 73, 78

"Nigger line," 59

No cure/no pay agreement, 72
Norman pin, 26, 29
Nozzle, Kort (*See* Kort nozzle)

Panama chock, 37, 82
Propeller design, 3-4
Propulsion, 3
Pump, auxiliary, 8
Push knee, 60-61

Quarter line, 36, 38

Ratchet, 59, 61
Refloating, 71
Rescue, 71-78
Rigging, tugboat, 16
Rudder design, 3-4

Salvage, 71-78
   costs, 72
   search pattern, schematic, 76
Shackles, 16, 24, 55
   screw-pin, 23
   thimbles and sockets, 23
Ship work, 30-40
Shockline, 52
Signals, whistle, 38
Single-screw tug (*See* Tug)
Spool, 59
Springline, 38, 41, 42, 44, 48, 52
Stack knee, 61
Steam engine, 2
Steam tug (*See* Tug, steam)
Sternline, 41, 43, 48, 61
Surge pennant, 16, 52

Tow
   boats, schematic, 7
   breaking, 48-52
   gear, 3 (*See also* Gear)
   hook, 40
   line, 36, 46, 48, 49
   making, 48-52
   span, 24
   straps, 26, 27, 41, 44
     schematic, 40
   tandem, 53-58
Towing board, 25
Towing tips, 87-91
   log entry, 88
Transmission, power, 3
Tug, 6-10, 65-70
   crew, 2

developments, 3-4
harbor, 30
horsepower, 6, 8-9
    performance table, 9
inland, 59-64
"in notch," 84
requirements, 2-3
single-screw, 6
size, 2, 6
steam, ii, 1
twin-screw, 6, 38, 81
types, schematic, 7
ventilation, 67
Twin-screw tug (*See* Tug)

Wall Rope Company, 18

Wheelhouse, 8, 31
Wijsberg Company, 71
Winch, 15, 19-20, 49, 61
    anchor, 79
    double-drum, 52, 53, 55, 81
    triple-drum, 53
Wire
    backing, 60
    breast, 60
    eye, 59
    face, 60, 62
    fore and aft, 60
    scissor, 60
    stern, 60
Working lines, 16, 17, 19, 27
    strength, fiber rope, table, 18